No One Else

is

Lawrence!

No One Else
is Lawrence!

A dozen of D. H. Lawrence's best poems
with introduction and commentary by
Doug Beardsley
& Al Purdy

Harbour
Publishing

Published by
Harbour Publishing
Box 219
Madeira Park, BC V0N 2H0

Cover artwork by Martin Nichols, Lionheart Graphics.
Front cover illustration from an original artwork by D.H. Lawrence
Page design and layout by David Lee Communications

We acknowledge the financial support of the Government of Canada through the Book Publishing Industry Development Program and the Province of British Columbia through the British Columbia Arts Council for our publishing activities.

Canadian Cataloguing in Publication Data

Beardsley, Doug, 1941–
    No one else is Lawrence!

    ISBN 1-55017-194-1

    1. Lawrence, D.H. (Donald Herbert), 1885–1930—Criticism and interpretation. I. Purdy, Al, 1918– II. Title.
PR6023.A93Z567 1998   821'.912   C98-910643-8

THE CANADA COUNCIL | LE CONSEIL DES ARTS
FOR THE ARTS | DU CANADA
SINCE 1957 | DEPUIS 1957

Contents

To:

Eurithe & Lin

out of the goodness of their hearts

Among the cypresses
To sit with pure, slim, long-nosed,
Evil-called, sensitive Etruscans, naked except for their boots;
To be able to smile back at them
And exchange the lost kiss
And come to dark connection.

    — *D.H.L.*

Acknowledgements

We would like to thank Laurence Pollinger Limited, and Heather Chalcroft, for their permission to publish the Lawrence poems. We would also like to thank the Canada Council. Special thanks to Lisa Power for her invaluable help, and to the people at The Waddling Dog, who bestowed on us the gift of silence.

Introductions:

Al Purdy

WHY THESE DOZEN POEMS OF D.H. LAWRENCE, and why these discussions between two friends of like mind about Lawrence?

Lawrence's genius has long been obscured by the brilliance and fame of his novels and essays, especially *Lady Chatterly's Lover*. "Oh that's the guy who wrote the sexy book with all those four-letter words" is liable to be the first comment one hears. "Wasn't he convicted of pornography?" is the second. The answer is yes to both those questions. And so was James Joyce, so have been a host of other writers whose names live, while those of their judges and accusers fade without even an echo.

Lawrence's critics have accused him of just about every sin in the book; his admirers are equally single-minded in their praise. But let's ignore both criti cs and admirers and look at the poems. At his very best, Lawrence's poems are unequaled. In the animal poems especially, the reader has joined the writer and leaped into the head of a kangaroo, has forgotten entirely that he/she is reading a few words on a page and becomes part of a trilogy consisting of reader, kangaroo, and above all, Lawrence.

In Italy a she-goat is climbing a low-growing almond tree: "like some horrid hairy God the Father in a William Blake imagination." One is stopped in his/her tracks by that line. How could anyone write it? There's a wild leap of the earthbound mind about it; link a hundred poets together with telepathy, and all of them together couldn't think of it. But there he is: God the Father without a depilatory inside the mind of long-dead William Blake, and yourself fascinated by it all.

Forget the nonsense you've read and heard about Lawrence; misconceptions are like a brain-eating disease. You have to read things for yourself, and not take anyone else's opinion, including ours. You have to voyage with the brain yourself, and these are far places of the imagination:

Nobody stuffs the world in at the eyes
The optic heart must venture
—thus saith Margaret Avison, and she speaks true.

Doug Beardsley

FATHER WAS BORN ON THE MIDLAND RAILWAY LINE above a pub in the town of Kimberley, three miles southeast of Lawrence's Eastwood, six miles northwest of Nottingham. I'd like to believe this explains my deep affinity for Lawrence, but there's another reason.

In grade ten I had an English teacher, a Mrs. Lampert. Our textbook had an enticing Mediterranean cover, but the same could not be said of its contents. This was the mid-1950s in cosmopolitan Montreal, but the book was stuffed with imitative Romantic and Neo-Georgian fluff designed to kill any reader's interest in poetry. My friend George Vlahos and I had convinced each other that there were only two true-blue poems here worthy of that name. His favourite was Auden's "Musée des Beaux Arts." Mine was Lawrence's "Snake."

In our teenage arrogance we slouched toward Mrs. Lampert, requesting that we take these two poems in class. When asked why, we responded like a Greek chorus, saying that these were the *only* two poems in the book. "No," said Mrs. Lampert. "Why not?" we asked, our jaws jutting toward her menacingly, our faces set in twin smirks like masks. "Because I don't understand them," she replied. "Poems aren't about meaning," we exclaimed triumphantly. "But, if you feel this way, *we'd* be glad to teach them in class." I never understood how she could have refused our generous offer. Or if this incident played any role in both of us soon after dropping out of school.

Eastwood is still uneasy about Lawrence. In 1971, while visiting relatives there, I happened to meet a very old man—probably an ex-miner—whose wife used to sit the wee Lawrence on her knee and take him for walks when he was a small boy. The old man told me: "After Lawrence left, Jessie Chambers moved in up there, ay, just a block away from Lynn Croft. I remember Jessie telling me wife 'He was just a sex-maniac, ay'" and the old miner's eyes went slightly crazy, as if he could almost see the dismembered bodies of young virgins Lawrence had hacked up.

The book you hold in your hands came about as the result of dozens of lunches over a three-year period. We began by discussing poetry, then poems, then the best poems of our time. We kept an anthology of these "best" poems, though it grew slowly, rather like the interest in a bank account. To say it was difficult to "get in" is an understatement. Stakes were high. We'd read a poet a week. The great poets of our century were represented by two or three poems; in the uppermost echelons Yeats had five or six.

Lawrence had twelve. We were nervous. How could this be? Were we suggesting that Lawrence was twice as good as Yeats? This was not only not possible, it was not permitted. Yet there it was.

And here it is. Such a different book. I'm certain nothing like it has been done.

Our wish is to turn and return the reader to Lawrence's best work, particularly the creatures, reptiles, and animals in *Birds, Beasts and Flowers*. This is the book to read first. Might I suggest that the commentaries be read the same way poems are read: one or two at a time?

Finally, I'd like to say how much we enjoyed making this book.

Victoria, BC
March 17, 1998

Kangaroo

In the northern hemisphere
Life seems to leap at the air, or skim under the wind
Like stags on rocky ground, or pawing horses, or springy scut-tailed
  rabbits.

Or else rush horizontal to charge at the sky's horizon,
Like bulls or bisons or wild pigs.

Or slip like water slippery towards its ends,
As foxes, stoats, and wolves, and prairie dogs.

Only mice, and moles, and rats, and badgers, and beavers, and perhaps
  bears
Seem belly-plumbed to the earth's mid-navel.
Or frogs that when they leap come flop, and flop to the centre of the
  earth.

But the yellow antipodal Kangaroo, when she sits up,
Who can unseat her, like a liquid drop that is heavy, and just touches
  earth.

The downward drip.
The down-urge.
So much denser than cold-blooded frogs.

Delicate mother Kangaroo
Sitting up there rabbit-wise, but huge, plumb-weighted,
And lifting her beautiful slender face, oh! so much more gently and
  finely-lined than a rabbit's, or than a hare's,
Lifting her face to nibble at a round white peppermint drop, which she
  loves, sensitive mother Kangaroo.

Her sensitive, long, pure-bred face.
Her full antipodal eyes, so dark,

So big and quiet and remote, having watched so many empty dawns in
    silent Australia.

Her little loose hands, and drooping Victorian shoulders.
And then her great weight below the waist, her vast pale belly
With a thin young yellow little paw hanging out, and straggle of a long
    thin ear, like ribbon,
Like a funny trimming to the middle of her belly, thin little dangle of an
    immature paw, and one thin ear.

Her belly, her big haunches
And in addition, the great muscular python-stretch of her tail.

There, she shan't have any more peppermint drops.
So she wistfully, sensitively sniffs the air, and then turns, goes off in slow
    and sad leaps

On the long flat skis of her legs,
Steered and propelled by that steel-strong snake of a tail.

Stops again, half turns, inquisitive to look back.
While something stirs quickly in her belly, and a lean little face comes
    out, as from a window,
Peaked and a bit dismayed,
Only to disappear again quickly away from the sight of the world, to
    snuggle down in the warmth,
Leaving the trail of a different paw hanging out.

Still she watches with eternal, cocked wistfulness!
How full her eyes are, like the full, fathomless, shining eyes of an
    Australian black-boy
Who has been lost so many centuries on the margins of existence!

She watches with insatiable wistfulness.
Untold centuries of watching for something to come,
For a new signal from life, in that silent lost land of the South.

Where nothing bites but insects and snakes and the sun, small life.
Where no bull roared, no cow ever lowed, no stag cried, no leopard
 screeched, no lion coughed, no dog barked,
But all was silent save for parrots occasionally, in the haunted blue bush.

Wistfully watching, with wonderful liquid eyes.
And all her weight, all her blood, dripping sack-wise down towards the
 earth's centre,
And the live little-one taking in its paw at the door of her belly.

Leap then, and come down on the line that draws to the earth's deep,
 heavy centre.

Commentary • *Kangaroo*

P. Let's look at the lines: "In the northern hemisphere / life seems to leap at the air, or skim under the wind / like stags on rocky ground, or pawing horses, or springy scut-tailed rabbits / Or else rush horizontal, to charge at the sky's horizon."

B. That's not difficult. Already he's got us hooked.

P. The minute I read that years ago he had me. I realized then whatever I knew about Lawrence I didn't know very much before that.

B. I got the feeling when I first read Lawrence that whatever I knew about life I didn't know very much before this.

P. He doesn't humiliate you but he gives you the feeling that you can learn so much from him.

B. He has accessibility, he invites you in, as reader.

P. That's right. He does.

B. It's as if he's Virgil; he's your guide through life.

P. And this is a miner's son, a guy who grew up in the utmost poverty and he knows more than all the professors he ever came across.

B. He is in touch with the essence of life and he brings this immediacy to his common language . . .

P. And I have no idea how he did it, but he did do it.

B. That's the mystery, that's the miracle of these poems.

P. And that's what we're trying to talk about.

B. For me, it's the second line: "life seems to leap at the air," he's got me in the first half of his second line.

P. And the stanza that begins: "There, she shan't have any more peppermint drops . . . and then turns, goes off in slow and sad leaps." It sounds like a mother looking after her irresponsible child. And he's saying it about an animal, which is what makes it so strange to me. And the way he talks about Australia when he's talking about the kangaroo: "How full her eyes are, like the full, fathomless, shining eyes of an Australian black-boy / who has been lost so many centuries on the margins of existence! ... Untold centuries of watching for something to come, for a new signal from life, in that silent lost land of the South." I have never heard anybody speak about Australia that way. You would never write that in 1998; it was written in the 1920s. And it was like that then. Now, with television, this is not true any longer. But it was true then. And he makes you feel it.

B. I read through the poem and I get again those eight or ten lines that seem to connect Lawrence not only with the title of the poem, but seem to connect Lawrence with the earth. They put him and the kangaroo together — and therefore the reader — in the centre of the earth.

P. In the fourth stanza he seems to pull at the umbilical cord between himself and kangaroo.

B. And the umbilical cord that is the poem between Lawrence and reader.

P. Right. But it's much stronger between Lawrence and the kangaroo.

B. The man is at the centre of the earth's core, it's as if the poems are being written a thousand miles down. In the molten volcanic centre. That's where Lawrence is writing from. Look at the poem.

P. Aren't you rather taking away from the immediacy that we've said Lawrence has if he's writing from the earth's centre?

B. The kangaroo "belly-plumbed to the earth's mid-navel" in a way that Lawrence belly plumbs to the poem's centre and takes the reader with him. He's always talking about the kangaroo and the baby kangaroo ...

P. But he's talking to us.

B. He's talking about us too, he's encouraging the reader to "leap" too, that the reader's imagination — and life — leap upward with / like this animal, this poem. It's a kind of request.

P. And the critics in the 1920s and the 1930s didn't understand that. They couldn't appreciate that. A lot of famous critics condemned this poem, along with others.

B. That's because the critical mind, the critical sensibility, doesn't care about that, it doesn't care about life lived at this level. The critical mind has another job to do, it sits in its study in its comfortable chair and is intellectual. It doesn't care about—sometimes it doesn't even see—this kind of leaping. This imaginative leaping is the poet's concern. Robert Bly wrote a series of good essays on just this subject in the 1960s and 1970s. But, my God, here's Lawrence half a century earlier doing the thing. The man is like a woman in that he is so psychologically grounded in and to the earth, in and to the animals of the earth. The kangaroo is Lawrence and he invites us to experience that synthesis. It's an amazing achievement.

P. I think so.

B. And it's not something you can critically discuss in class. It's not criticism. What we're doing now is appreciation. Feeling. It's not applying the intellectuality of criticism. That's why the critics missed the poems we've included here. Because they're rare. And so special.

P. It describes a kangaroo in such a way as a kangaroo has never been described before.

There Are No Gods

There are no gods, and you can please yourself
have a game of tennis, go out in the car, do some shopping, sit and talk,
    talk, talk
with a cigarette browning your fingers.

There are no gods, and you can please yourself—
go and please yourself—

But leave me alone, leave me alone, to myself!
and then in the room, whose is the presence
that makes the air so still and lovely to me?

Who is it that softly touches the sides of my breast
and touches me over the heart
so that my heart beats soothed, soothed, soothed and at peace?

Who is it smoothes the bed-sheets like the cool
smooth ocean where the fishes rest on edge
in their own dream?

Who is it that clasps and kneads my naked feet, till they unfold,
till all is well, till all is utterly well? the lotus-lilies of the feet!

I tell you, it is no woman, it is no man, for I am alone.
And I fall asleep with the gods, the gods
that are not, or that are
according to the soul's desire,
like a pool into which we plunge, or do not plunge.

Commentary • *There Are No Gods*

P. "There Are No Gods" is as much a public poem as Lawrence ever wrote.

B. The first stanza is in the tone that Lawrence used in "Kangaroo" when he admonishes the animal.

P. But who's he talking to?

B. He's talking to all of us.

P. He's talking to himself as well.

B. Both.

P. Yes. Both. All.

B. There's something off-putting about that opening though.

P. It says to hell with it. You can please yourself, do what you like. I'm going to believe what I believe.

B. I'm going to believe what I've experienced. He's saying it is the experience that tells me it is true.

P. It's a simple poem.

B. We're having trouble talking about it and this is telling me something.

P. Yet, at the same time, he's expressing his own philosophy of art. His philosophy regarding the gods is the same philosophy he brings to the poems, is it not?

B. Can you expand on that?

P. The people who say there are no gods are the people who make rules—no, I don't want to say that . . .

B. You're suggesting that this is where the poems come from? That for the real poet, for the genius, for Lawrence, the poems come from some other source?

P. He is proving that there are gods to himself.

B. Because of the poetry.

P. He is demonstrating to himself that he is right.

B. Because of the poems.

P. Because he feels the presence of gods physically. He is right about the gods because of this truth. And that applies to the poems, as well, because he has abrogated all the rules of other people.

B. And the poems come from deep within the self. They also come from one's own experience, from external life.

P. Doug, it's going to be extremely humiliating if we ever find anybody else who's said much the same things as Lawrence who wrote blank verse and free verse poems. And I think some poets did. However, I just don't think that they can ever equal Lawrence.

B. I agree.

P. It seems to me he's saying that he's an individual and a god has touched him—or something very similar to a god . . .

B. But we're saying they touch him most when he's writing.

P. Yes, that's right.

B. That the poems are evidence of this "other" force.

P. As far as we're concerned, they are. He does not say that but, nevertheless, I think somehow he means it. "Who is it that softly touches . . . ?" When you're writing a poem you are about as free as is possible. I have a theory about writing and that is when you write a line there are hundreds or thousands of thoughts in your mind, they form like lightning in your head, and you must choose one out of all these. And you do. But, later, you are dissatisfied. And you must choose another. You go through the same process all over again. I think this is somehow what Lawrence is talking about here.

B. And that "plunging" into the pool he talks about in the last stanza is diving into the imaginative process, the collective unconscious, if one is really lucky. And there's water in the pool. And one resurfaces, naturally.

P. There's an ambiguity here though. He could be talking both about the gods and writing.

B. Yes, it's an intentional ambiguity or an unconscious one—it doesn't matter. We, as readers, are invited to plunge into the poem, or risk taking the plunge ourselves into the creative process.

P. And that penultimate stanza ending with "...the lotus-lilies of the feet," Jesus, that is beautiful phraseology.

B. I'm intrigued by "...the gods that are not, or that are / according to the soul's desire." It's according to the poet, Lawrence is saying here, it is the poet who conjures up the gods according to what he wants, according to the imaginative selection he makes, the choices you referred to earlier, the thousands of lightning strikes from which one has to choose.

P. That's a better way of describing it. And there are thousands of them, we don't know what goes on in the human mind. I believe that happens.

B. And we make these choices "according to the soul's desire." And he ends by saying this is "like a pool into which we plunge, or do not plunge." We don't have to go—and most people don't venture into that imaginative, creative world, they stay entirely in the world of the first stanza, they go out in the car and do some shopping. Lawrence has contempt for the real, external world, what he wants is the deep inner desires to be expressed and so Lawrence took the plunge in a way that few others have even dared. The creative artist takes the plunge in a way that most people don't even conceive of.

P. Yes, it's an allegory in that sense.

B. It's an interesting image.

P. Did he mean it that way, do you think?

B. I don't know, we can never know.

P. But it is.

B. Yes, of course. Let me put it this way, Al: it would be difficult not to read "There Are No Gods" in this way.

P. That it refers to poetry, it refers to the imagination.

B. Yes. And it's a powerful last image because here he uses water in a way that, in "Kangaroo," he kept using the centre of the earth. Here he's using another image that does the same thing, of reaching down, into the centre of the self ...

P. Except that the kangaroo does it naturally. We don't give the kangaroo any intelligence or any reason to do this except that it was its body, whereas here it's the mind.

B. But Lawrence is saying that the poet is like that too, like the kangaroo, the poet is in touch with these other forces.

P. Yes, but I mean the kangaroo is not—or is, but only in the sense that it is the kangaroo's physiognomy.

B. Yeah, but surely the point is that the animal is naturally in touch with forces?

P. Yes, I think you're right. I think I'm wrong there.

B. In the first stanza he points out that our normal lives are completely out of touch with these forces; indeed Lawrence found such a "normal" life abnormal because it moves us away from the very creative sources that the kangaroo naturally feels and to which it responds: the spontaneous, the intuitive, the imaginative leap, and so on.

P. We have these too, he's saying, if you can free your mind from all these preconceived trivialities.

B. If you can free your mind from the first stanza.

P. In a sense this poem is a cry of defiance. And Lawrence lived his life as an act of defiance. Which allowed him to say my bronchial tubes are giving me trouble, I do not have tuberculosis. It's not rational at all, it escapes rationality, and that's what Lawrence did, he escaped.

B. To extend the image of the last line, Lawrence is like a high diver, like Margaret Avison's "The Swimmer," like Layton's poem with the same title—which was probably inspired by Lawrence.

P. I don't think Lawrence prepared for that last line in this poem.

B. No, there's no previous image that prepares us for the water. However, there is the "smooth ocean" ... (and) "the fishes."

P. It's there because it's there in the totality of Lawrence's poems.

B. Does it then work for you as one of his great poems?

P. Yes, it does. Though I don't believe in the gods myself ...

B. But he did.

P. But he did. He believed in the gods of imagination. And I believe in the gods of imagination. I believe in them, in the way Lawrence created himself, freed himself from all the fetters that are placed on us, on the human mind. We all know that we live two lives. That we live our public lives in which we talk to each other, live in a way so that we don't get arrested. We also live our private lives, released from all the fetters, in which we think very different thoughts.

B. And live different lives. And poetry does this.

P. And we get away with as much as we can, if we think it does not offend our morals, our personal morality.

B. And that's what the poet is doing in writing, which is a very private act. He or she is most free when writing.

P. That's right. Though there are, of course, places where the public morality touches the private morality.

B. But when we take that plunge into the imaginative world one leaves behind external realities.

P. Right. We are, in a sense, doing that right now.

B. Yes. We are diving into the pool of this poem. "There Are No Gods" is a poem about the imaginative process.

P. I agree completely. This can be said about so many of Lawrence's poems. There is a connection. Not that it's very obvious; but they all connect.

Snake

A snake came to my water-trough
On a hot, hot day, and I in pyjamas for the heat,
To drink there.

In the deep, strange-scented shade of the great dark carob-tree
I came down the steps with my pitcher
And must wait, must stand and wait, for there he was at the trough
    before me.

He reached down from a fissure in the earth-wall in the gloom
And trailed his yellow-brown slackness soft-bellied down, over the edge
    of the stone trough
And rested his throat upon the stone bottom,
And where the water had dripped from the tap, in a small clearness,
He sipped with his straight mouth,
Softly drank through his straight gums, into his slack long body,
Silently.

Someone was before me at my water-trough,
And I, like a second-comer, waiting.

He lifted his head from his drinking, as cattle do,
And looked at me vaguely, as drinking cattle do,
And flickered his two-forked tongue from his lips, and mused a moment,
And stopped and drank a little more,
Being earth-brown, earth-golden from the burning bowels of the earth
On the day of Sicilian July, with Etna smoking.

The voice of my education said to me
He must be killed,
For in Sicily the black, black snakes are innocent, the gold are venomous.

And voices in me said, If you were a man
You would take a stick and break him now, and finish him off.

But must I confess how I liked him,
How glad I was he had come like a guest in quiet, to drink at my
      water-trough
And depart peaceful, pacified, and thankless,
Into the burning bowels of this earth?

Was it cowardice, that I dared not kill him?
Was it perversity, that I longed to talk to him?
Was it humility, to feel so honoured?
I felt so honoured.

And yet those voices:
If you were not afraid, you would kill him!

And truly I was afraid, I was most afraid,
But even so, honoured still more
That he should seek my hospitality
From out the dark door of the secret earth.

He drank enough
And lifted his head, dreamily, as one who has drunken,
And flickered his tongue like a forked night on the air, so black,
Seeming to lick his lips,
And looked around like a god, unseeing, into the air,
And slowly turned his head,
And slowly, very slowly, as if thrice adream,
Proceeded to draw his slow length curving round
And climb again the broken bank of my wall-face.

And as he put his head into that dreadful hole,
And as he slowly drew up, snake-easing his shoulders, and entered
      farther,
A sort of horror, a sort of protest against his withdrawing into that
      horrid black hole,
Deliberately going into the blackness, and slowly drawing himself after,
Overcame me now his back was turned.

I looked round, I put down my pitcher,
I picked up a clumsy log
And threw it at the water-trough with a clatter.

I think it did not hit him,
But suddenly that part of him that was left behind convulsed in
     undignified haste,
Writhed like lightning, and was gone
Into the black hole, the earth-lipped fissure in the wall-front,
At which, in the intense still noon, I stared with fascination.

And immediately I regretted it.
I thought how paltry, how vulgar, what a mean act!
I despised myself and the voices of my accursed human education.

And I thought of the albatross,
And I wished he would come back, my snake.

For he seemed to me again like a king,
Like a king in exile, uncrowned in the underworld,
Now due to be crowned again.

And so, I missed my chance with one of the lords
Of life.
And I have something to expiate:
A pettiness.

Commentary • *Snake*

P. It's sort of a short story, if you like. There are several reasons why Lawrence has to wait at the water trough. It's a poisonous snake because the yellow ones are poisonous, the gold ones venomous as he says. But Lawrence doesn't want to kill the snake because he regards it as an individual and as something that has its own identity, but his education tells him to do it. Although it's more than education because when you see a snake you shudder a little bit along the backbone—I do anyway. You don't always want to kill it, but you don't want to have very much to do with it. So that was part of the way he was feeling too. I find the whole poem is a story, a very good story, but it's more than that of course.

B. There's something going on here that we haven't seen before. And it may be why "Snake" is so anthologized while other poems of his are chosen less often, and are not nearly as well known. You remember how we talked about Lawrence becoming one with the animal ...

P. He doesn't here.

B. ... or with the thing he is describing. But here he's separated from the snake, he's in his human self and he's completely in the poem.

P. You're not going to make yourself one with a snake; it doesn't seem likely.

B. But there's a further division. Lawrence is entirely in the poem but he's split in two. He's divided about what to do about the snake. His intelligent self wants to kill the thing, but his intuitive self makes him virtually akin to the snake.

P. Well, it's a poisonous snake and they're dangerous, as you know.

B. But I guess they're only dangerous if you come to them. They probably wouldn't attack you for no reason.

P. Some snakes do. This one probably wouldn't.

B. Lawrence is like Hamlet, the protagonist here is a Hamletian figure, undecided about what to do, whether to take action or not. That division of soul that is occurring here is the same kind that occurs in Shakespeare.

And he's torn between the voice of education, the voice of reason that tells him he should strike the snake and kill it, and another voice . . .

P. It's the voice of the snake . . .

B. . . . and another unconscious voice that sees the snake as a god and lord and master of his realm, a thing that should be honoured and left alone. And he doesn't know what to do, which voice to obey.

P. No, he doesn't seem to.

B. The snake has its own divinity. It's clear that it should be honoured.

P. Why should it be honoured?

B. It's divine.

P. Why is it divine?

B. Because he's calling it a god, he's giving it divine-like attributes.

P. But that doesn't make it a god.

B. He's seeing it that way.

P. He's seeing it that way, yeah.

B. So he doesn't know what to do.

P. I believe he's also thinking of a passage in his essay, "Love Was Once a Little Boy," seeing the snake as an individual, though he's carrying it much further, of course.

B. Yes, he's saying the snake has its own individuality, and it should be respected as such.

P. Is he thinking of the albatross in "The Ancient Mariner"?

B. It must be the Coleridge poem. So, in the end he wishes that the snake would come back—like the albatross?

P. Probably. Also, at the beginning, there's ownership; it's his water trough and he's waiting on the steps with a pitcher. He's a little irritated about that. Also the snake is poisonous. You must not forget the snake is poisonous.

B. It's his water trough and, did you notice at the end of the poem it's my snake?

P. Oh, yes, he's changing his view of it.

B. But it's also ownership. "And I wished he would come back, my snake."

P. Yes, well, there is the natural life in the world to which Lawrence has more feeling for than he has for human life perhaps.

B. Oh, yes. And what he's trying to do here in this unusual poem—unusual because he is so much in it—is to show our ambivalence toward nature and animals.

P. I'd like to know what he means by that reference to his education: does he mean because he knows the snake is poisonous? Or that people generally fear snakes?

B. I'm going to poison you, Al—with a poisonous snake. I think he's talking about something deeper. A state of mind that calls out for us to lash out and kill the snake.

P. Would you refer to that as "education"?

B. It's an odd word to use in this context but it's the conventional, human response. Based on fear. It's the voice of man in society as opposed to the spontaneous self that feels for the snake, the spontaneous self that Lawrence worshipped.

P. He gives himself several alternatives.

B. Like Hamlet, who gives himself a number of reasons why he shouldn't kill his uncle.

P. I doubt like hell he's thinking of Hamlet.

B. No, but I am.

P. He's thinking of the albatross.

B. At the end of the poem, yes. But, earlier, where he lists the reasons why he wants to kill the snake it strikes me as the same kind of procrastination—the battle between the two senses of self that Hamlet experienced.

P. Uh uh. The poem hinges on "the voices of my ... education" and he's changing, he's saying "I'm not going to go by that anymore, I'm going to go by my instincts."

B. That's right.

P. That's just about what Lawrence always says.

B. He always worshipped the instinctual. The reptile represents that instinctive, primordial urge. Education takes one away from real life. The protagonist here has a choice: he can kill this thing—

P. Or what?

B. Worship it?

P. Not really. He calls it a king but it's not worship per se.

B. Honour it?

P. Honour it in his mind perhaps.

B. Respect its place in the whole scheme of things.

P. Auden and even Eliot must have admired this. They admired much about Lawrence, and said so. Along with things they didn't like—or thought they didn't like.

B. In the end Lawrence identifies with the snake. The instinctual side of him wins out.

P. He's still going to stay away. He's going to respect it, honour it, but from a distance.

B. From a distance. Damn right. The albatross was hung around the guy's neck in Coleridge's poem, but he's not going to wear this one.

P. No, he sure isn't.

B. By throwing the stick at the end he's missed a chance to what? To communicate? To become one with it? Or simply to sit and observe it?

P. Ah, yes, that. The pettiness is important too.

B. The pettiness is the urge he had to kill him, the urge to behave in that human way, to behave like a man.

P. That's right, it was something that it wasn't necessary to do.

B. It'd be like if we went outside to your stream in the backyard and clubbed those otters.

P. Oh, you'd never catch 'em. Those otters are like flashes of light.

B. Lawrence is able to capture the experience, what Auden referred to as the transparency of the thing.

P. Which is what a lot of other poets/writers do not do. The reader is often waylaid, delayed, trapped, set aside by something—whatever it might be in the poem. The murkiness of it.

Man and Bat

When I went into my room, at mid-morning,
Say ten o'clock . . .
My room, a crash-box over that great stone rattle
The Via de' Bardi . . .

When I went into my room at mid-morning
Why? . . . a bird!

A bird
Flying round the room in insane circles.

In insane circles!
. . . A bat!

A disgusting bat
At mid-morning! . . .

Out! Go out!

Round and round and round
With a twitchy, nervous, intolerable flight,
And a neurasthenic lunge,
And an impure frenzy;
A bat, big as a swallow!

Out, out of my room!

The venetian shutters I push wide
To the free, calm upper air;
Loop back the curtains . . .

Now out, out from my room!

So to drive him out, flicking with my white handkerchief: *Go!*
But he will not.

Round and round and round
In an impure haste,
Fumbling, a beast in air,
And stumbling, lunging and touching the walls, the bell-wires
About my room!

Always refusing to go out into the air
Above that crash-gulf of the Via de' Bardi,
Yet blind with frenzy, with cluttered fear.

At last he swerved into the window bay,
But blew back, as if an incoming wind blew him in again.
A strong inrushing wind.

And round and round and round!
Blundering more insane, and leaping, in throbs, to clutch at a corner,
At a wire, at a bell-rope:
On and on, watched relentless by me, round and round in my room,
Round and round and dithering with tiredness and haste and increasing
        delirium
Flicker-splashing round my room.

I would not let him rest;
Not one instant cleave, cling like a blot with his breast to the wall
In an obscure corner.
Not an instant!

I flicked him on,
Trying to drive him through the window.

Again he swerved into the window bay
And I ran forward, to frighten him forth.
But he rose, and from a terror worse than me he flew past me
Back into my room, and round, round, round in my room

Clutch, cleave, stagger,
Dropping about the air
Getting tired.

Something seemed to blow him back from the window
Every time he swerved at it;
Back on a strange parabola, then round, round, dizzy in my room.

He *could* not go out;
I also realised . . .
It was the light of day which he could not enter,
Any more than I could enter the white-hot door of a blast furnace.

He could not plunge into the daylight that streamed at the window.
It was asking too much of his nature.

Worse even than the hideous terror of me with my handkerchief
Saying: *Out, go out!* . . .
Was the horror of white daylight in the window!

So I switched on the electric light, thinking: *Now
The outside will seem brown* . . .

But no.
The outside did not seem brown.
And he did not mind the yellow electric light.

Silent!
He was having a silent rest.
But never!
Not in my room.

Round and round and round
Near the ceiling as if in a web
Staggering;
Plunging, falling out of the web,
Broken in heaviness,

Lunging blindly,
Heavier;
And clutching, clutching for one second's pause,
Always, as if for one drop of rest,
One little drop.

And I!
Never, I say ...
Get out!

Flying slower,
Seeming to stumble, to fall in air.
Blind-weary.

Yet never able to pass the whiteness of light into freedom ...
A bird would have dashed through, come what might.

Fall, sink, lurch, and round and round
Flicker, flicker-heavy;
Even wings heavy:
And cleave in a high corner for a second, like a clot, also a prayer.

But no.
Out, you beast.

Till he fell in a corner, palpitating, spent.
And there, a clot, he squatted and looked at me.
With sticking-out, beady-berry eyes, black,
And improper derisive ears,
And shut wings,
And brown, furry body.

Brown, nut-brown, fine fur!
But it might as well have been hair on a spider; thing
With long, black-paper ears.

So, a dilemma!
He squatted there like something unclean.

No, he must not squat, nor hang, obscene, in my room!

Yet nothing on earth will give him courage to pass the sweet fire of day.

What then?
Hit him and kill him and throw him away?

Nay,
I didn't create him.
Let the God that created him be responsible for his death ...
Only, in the bright day, I will not have this clot in my room.

Let the God who is maker of bats watch with them in their unclean
       corners ...
I admit a God in every crevice,
But not bats in my room;
Nor the God of bats, while the sun shines.

So out, out you brute! ...
And he lunged, flight-heavy, away from me, sideways, *a sghembo!*
And round and round and round my room, a clot with wings
Impure even in weariness.

Wings dark skinny and flapping the air,
Lost their flicker.
Spent.

He fell again with a little thud
Near the curtain on the floor.
And there lay.

Ah, death, death,
You are no solution!
Bats must be bats.

Only life has a way out.
And the human soul is fated to wide-eyed responsibility
In life.

So I picked him up in a flannel jacket,
Well covered, lest he should bite me.
For I would have had to kill him if he'd bitten me, the impure one . . .
And he hardly stirred in my hand, muffled up.

Hastily, I shook him out of the window.

And away he went!
Fear craven in his tail.
Great haste, and straight, almost bird straight above the Via de' Bardi.
Above that crash-gulf of exploding whips,
Towards the Borgo San Jacopo.

And now, at evening, as he flickers over the river
Dipping with petty triumphant flight, and tittering over the sun's
        departure,
I believe he chirps, pipistrello, seeing me here on this terrace writing:
There he sits, the long loud one!
But I am greater than he . . .
I escaped him . . . .

Commentary • *Man and Bat*

B. I'm struck immediately by how Lawrence sets this, how the natural elemental energy of the bat is trapped in Lawrence's room. He wants the bat out of his room but the bat is trapped and the trap is civilization.

P. Well, the bat would get out if it knew how. You're being symbolic.

B. The poem is symbolic. It's pretty hard to miss. The bat has mistakenly flown into man's domain. The bat is filled with terror.

P. Lawrence terrifies the bat but he doesn't terrify the mosquito. The mosquito is evil; the bat is merely disgusting. He's saying something different here. He gives the bat credit for his individuality, but says he didn't create him, let the god that created him be responsible for his death. And that's unusual. Lawrence will not kill the bat.

B. I'm stuck on one line. When he wants the bat to leave he says in the middle of the poem: "It was asking too much of his nature." That's so beautiful.

P. Why is it beautiful?

B. Because it's an acute observation.

P. But we know a bat can't go out into the daylight.

B. But to put it this way, so simply, almost a commonplace and yet it has a sense of nobility about it. This is what Auden meant by Lawrence's "transparency." The absolute rightness of the thing. That's all. It's everything.

P. It almost seems an accident and Lawrence is *not* transparent. The poem seems like a soliloquy; in fact it's so many different things at once. The whole thing is addressed to himself.

B. I've never found anyone in poetry able to use language quite like this and who achieves such transparency.

P. Other people would say that Whitman had the same transparency but to me Whitman is simple-minded by comparison. Lawrence achieves a drama. Whitman is talking about something that is not in the room with him, not present ... Lawrence is far more immediate.

B. I was just going to say that Lawrence captures the immediate experience . . .

P. What he talks about when he refers to "poetry of the present" . . .

B. . . . whereas Whitman seems to be talking in generalities.

P. Whitman is talking in grandiose generalities.

B. He wants to embrace all of America and he's so damn conscious of doing this. It's a conscious effort with Whitman; with Lawrence the poems are coming from a deeper source so he just lets them come.

P. Lawrence just does it. Whitman is without the informing intelligence that permeates everything Lawrence says.

B. Whitman doesn't have the direct accessibility to the unconscious that Lawrence has.

P. It's as if Whitman makes it up as a philosophy.

B. He's very conscious of doing this for America. Whitman's work sometimes seems willed. I'm interested that in the middle of the poem Lawrence tells us that a bird would have dashed out into the daylight. He makes the distinction between a bird and the behaviour of the bat. The bird has the instinct to leave.

P. I don't agree. I've seen a bird get similarly trapped.

B. But far from fearing the daylight the bird seeks the daylight.

P. However, we see this room at night. But I think there's a crisis in this poem which occurs four or five stanzas from the end when Lawrence says, "Nay, I didn't create him." This, again, takes us back to "Love Was Once A Little Boy." "Let the god that created him be responsible for his death." Much of that essay has to do with the independence, the difference of all created things. Especially living things. "Let the god that created him be responsible for his death." I've never been exactly sure how religious Lawrence was.

B. He's deeply religious but not in any orthodox sense. I was struck by his incessant repetition of the fact that the bat was in "*my* room" (italics mine). Fifteen times and twice in one line is a bit much. Another example of Lawrence sledgehammering us over the head in case we might just miss it, I guess. But the bat has invaded man's territory, to be sure. So he has to get him out in order to save him because the bat has no place in man's world.

P. He isn't comfortable in it, he's terrorized by it. He's a prisoner, and he knows it.

B. That line "Let the god that created him ..." takes us forward to "Fish" and the line "I didn't know his god." Here he's saying I don't know this god either, there's another god that's responsible here, not my god. Wow, talk about other worlds ...

P. Well, or a god who has a very large personality, let us say, and can express sympathy for all the creatures of this earth. This is something to say.

B. But what he's saying is there is a god beyond our god.

P. He believed in many gods. He believed in the god of the Etruscans, but there were others as well.

B. The key phrase here is surely "I admit a God in every crevice." There is a God other than our God and it's the former that is being called for, almost summoned here. And it's a God that Lawrence doesn't know—in the same way he doesn't know it in "Fish." It's a primordial God and there is no space for it in the room. Man has no place for such a God as this.

P. There are certain animals in the world for which one feels an extreme distaste—dislike allied with fear.

B. Is that because they're primordial and they remind us of an earlier life? Ours?

P. I doubt it. I think they remind us of what we can't guard against in ourselves the way we can guard against some animals—it's very difficult to guard against snakes or bats, for instance. If you're asleep a bat will come up and suck your blood if he's a certain kind of bat. And a snake is a wiggly thing on the ground and he makes me uneasy. He's so far away from our hands and our head—our self-protection. Kicking a poisonous snake would be extremely dangerous.

B. Maybe they unconsciously remind us of an earlier, cozier earth-centred existence.

P. It's possible, it's possible, but I think it's something even more basic than that. I'm sure other people have tried to get at this. That there's something nasty about them. I can remember as a child somebody threw a snake at me—caught me around the neck—I was terrified for a second.

B. I think Lawrence is wrestling with some early ancestral life here, one we now shun. Lawrence identifies with these creatures because he's asking us to recover an aspect of that elemental life in our own lives.

P. Lawrence talks about this earlier world you think he's trying to get across here in a very immediate way. This is a poem of action all the way through.

B. He's acting like a man. And like a man he says at the end of the poem that if the bat had bit him he would have had to kill it but if the bat doesn't bite him ...

P. He would have been angered in the first instance.

B. And so the bat goes ...

P. "Above that crash-gulf of exploding whips." What are the "exploding whips"?

B. I took it as the sea tides. Though he is in Florence.

P. And the "Via de' Bardi" is a road. Beyond the road?

B. I took it that it would be the road to the coast. The sea's crash.

P. But he's not at the sea because he "flickers over the river."

B. He can fly a long distance awfully fast! I would guess the "Borgo San Jacopo" to be a mountain range but I don't know. In central Italy you can have a city, mountain range and the sea all within a few miles of each other. I don't think there's a difficulty of geography here. We can trust Lawrence ... can't we? What do you make of the end Al, where the bat chirps how great it is because it escaped man yet we know that man makes that escape possible.

P. Perhaps he's now placing himself in the same category as the bat. As if for awhile they were rivals in the room, enemies ... Obviously, Lawrence is placing his own ironic words in the bat's mouth.

B. But the bat hasn't got it right. The bat is incapable of freeing itself from man's world, except by chance. What the bat says is good as far as it goes, but it's learned nothing.

P. As far as Lawrence is concerned, the bat has learned something.

B. What?

P. That he is greater than the man because he escaped him.

B. He's learned something, even if it isn't true!

P. It's a joke but, at the same time, if the bat could think it might think that. But Lawrence placed those words there. It's funny as hell when you think of it.

B. Lawrence had a wonderful comedic sensibility, yet it's seldom mentioned.

P. Imagine writing an epic poem about a bat.

The Mosquito

When did you start your tricks
Monsieur?

What do you stand on such high legs for?
Why this length of shredded shank
You exaltation?

Is it so that you shall lift your centre of gravity upwards
And weigh no more than air as you alight upon me,
Stand upon me weightless, you phantom?

I heard a woman call you the Winged Victory
In sluggish Venice.
You turn your head towards your tail, and smile.

How can you put so much devilry
Into that translucent phantom shred
Of a frail corpus?

Queer, with your thick wings and your streaming legs
How you wail like a heron, or a dull clot of air,
A nothingness.

Yet what an aura surrounds you;
Your evil little aura, prowling, and casting a numbness on my mind.

That is your trick, your bit of filthy magic:
Invisibility, and the anaesthetic power
To deaden my attention in your direction.

But I know your game now, streaky sorcerer.
Queer how you stalk and prowl the air
In circles and evasions, enveloping me,
Ghoul on wings
Winged Victory.

Settle, and stand on long thin shanks
Eyeing me sideways, and cunningly conscious that I am aware,
You speck.

I hate the way you lurch off sideways into air
Having read my thoughts against you.

Come then, let us play at unawares,
And see who wins in this sly game of bluff,
Man or mosquito.

You don't know that I exist, and I don't know that you exist.
Now then!

It is your trump
It is your hateful little trump
You pointed fiend,
Which shakes my sudden blood to hatred of you:
It is your small, high, hateful bugle in my ear.

Why do you do it?
Surely it is bad policy.

They say you can't help it.

If that is so, then I believe a little in Providence protecting the innocent.
But it sounds so amazingly like a slogan,
A yell of triumph as you snatch my scalp.

Blood, red blood
Super-magical
Forbidden liquor.

I behold you stand
For a second enspasmed in oblivion,
Obscenely ecstasied
Sucking live blood,
My blood.

Such silence, such suspended transport,
Such gorging,
Such obscenity of trespass.

You stagger
As well as you may.
Only your accursed hairy frailty
Your own imponderable weightlessness
Saves you, wafts you away on the very draught my anger makes in its
    snatching.

Away with a paean of derision
You winged blood-drop.

Can I not overtake you?
Are you one too many for me,
Winged Victory?
Am I not mosquito enough to out-mosquito you?

Queer, what a big stain my sucked blood makes
Beside the infinitesimal faint smear of you!
Queer, what a dim dark smudge you have disappeared into!

Commentary • *The Mosquito*

P. Lawrence talks about mosquitoes very differently than he talks about animals. He invents words for mosquitoes: "shredded shank ... you exaltation." Exaltation is obviously imagination—which is very different from the way he treats animals.

B. Here he seems to be inventing the creature he's writing about, imagining it into existence, his existence. Rather than trying to get to the essence of its being, as it were.

P. Lawrence had some personal feelings against the mosquito, which causes him to invent this invective—this *is* invective that Lawrence is using.

B. In one of the middle stanzas he describes him as "you speck"; it's almost like "dreck," like it's dung, worthless. The invented imagined hate that he sets up is highly unusual for Lawrence. He's the devil's advocate here.

P. Which makes me wonder, is he being bitter at the time or is he putting it in afterwards? Is he being plagued by mosquitoes while he's writing this poem?

B. In that short couplet that ends: "Having read my thoughts against you" it is clear that the mosquito has that essence of pure being that Lawrence wanted us human beings to rediscover, to recover. It understands how the man is thinking. Lawrence is always writing about a lost time, a once-upon-a-time paradise when we were totally in touch with our collective unconscious.

P. What we should do is get some mosquitoes in this room and let them bite us and we'll discuss the poem while getting bitten. And see how we'd look at it. However, there's a quality about a mosquito of invisibility, which is what Lawrence is also talking about here. If you've ever been in a bedroom, and a mosquito attacks you as soon as the light goes out (though I assume the light is on here), the mosquito simply disappears into the darkness, you don't know where the damn thing is. Lawrence conveys that feeling. And he also ascribes such evils, such nastiness, to the mosquito, which the mosquito does not possess. It's all in Lawrence's head.

B. He scapegoats the mosquito, it's all projection and, in that regard, it's a very unusual poem of Lawrence's. It's an unusual perspective for him.

P. The qualities he gives that mosquito! And it takes, as he says, "my blood"; how indignant he is. This is a poem full of indignation. Surely he knows what he's doing, he knows how he looks, he looks silly!

B. But he doesn't mind, Lawrence doesn't mind being silly.

P. No, he doesn't mind at all. And that's the way to write a poem.

B. He's so astonishingly open, he's so willing to risk, to let himself go. He wasn't afraid of what he'd find. He was certain of himself.

P. Why does he call the mosquito "the Winged Victory"? The Winged Victory is a rather magnificent sculpture in Paris and comparing a mosquito to the Winged Victory . . . ?

B. Maybe he's writing this in the south of France having just come from Paris. It would have taken no more than that.

P. There is no more incongruous likeness.

B. Surely he intends that incongruity. And, in the end here, unlike "Snake," where he honours the reptile, he squashes the damn thing.

P. We'd all squash the damn thing.

B. Here the more manly, the more human instinct, the "education" of us all, wins out. He kills the creature. Lawrence had the amazing ability to look at life from a wide variety of perspectives. He doesn't approach everything in the same way.

P. He's not like one of those people who think that killing anything at all is evil. Bugs are exempted from our general goodwill toward the animal.

B. They are for Lawrence, that's for sure.

P. They are for me too. I will kill a mosquito or a flea or anything else like that.

B. Here, unlike "Snake," he does the thing in.

P. The snake—which is a much more dangerous creature—somehow seems allied to the earth. It has a quality about it that makes it very different from the mosquito. How does one say it? Allied to the earth is as good a way of saying it as any.

B. I know Al, it's poisonous. Here he gives it evil properties ... he says the mosquito is "nothing" and yet, paradoxically, it's "something" at the same time.

P. What wonderful lines: "such suspended transport, such gorging, such obscenity of trespass." It's so wonderful and it's funny as hell too.

B. The mosquito is something different from us.

P. When he describes the thing as "obscenely ecstasied ... sucking live blood" it sounds as if it's having an evil orgasm.

B. All the poems are attempts to get at the very soul of the thing he's describing, except here the soul of the thing is a creation of Lawrence's imagination. He's created this thing, he's a god (Lawrence would have loved that). The evil attributes which he attributes to the mosquito don't exist.

P. It's as much invective in one poem as I've ever read. He's done this before in some of the "Pansies" where he attacks the people who outlawed his paintings—but not to this extent.

B. Not nearly so imaginatively.

P. This is simply all-out. Without using a single swear word, not a cuss word.

B. It's an imaginative conception.

P. We're raving, you know.

B. Maybe it's about time we did. Rave about Lawrence.

P. You ever gone after a mosquito? I've taken one of those Raid cans and gone all over the room, closed the room off, gone out, come back much later and the damn thing is still there. Why does he call the mosquito "Monsieur"? Why not call it Mister?

B. It's a French mosquito?

P. It doesn't seem French to me. Is it a token of respect? Throughout the rest of the poem he has no respect for it. Except in its abilities to annoy him.

B. But Lawrence is well aware of the jocular tone of the poem, of course, he's aware of the comedy of it all.

P. The whole poem is a complete exclamation. Don't forget too that Lawrence was rather like a mosquito himself; he was very thin. So when he asks "Am I not mosquito enough to out-mosquito you?" he's thinking of himself! Lawrence is flying through the air, chasing a mosquito! As he grew older he grew more and more like a mosquito. He was so ill.

B. He had TB.

P. He had avian TB, which is a particular kind. Maybe it's mosquito TB.

B. Hence the mosquito as the ultimate evil, a purveyor of death.

P. A mosquito gives all sorts of diseases. Can't you just see Lawrence flying through the air, chasing a mosquito, with his thin shanks.

B. Easily. Particularly after this poem.

P. When you examine a poem like this you give it far more attention than you do in a casual reading.

B. This is the way a poem should be read. With this kind of attention.

P. He does all this without thinking about it very much. He's simply enjoying himself.

B. But what invention.

Elephant

You go down shade to the river, where naked men sit on flat brown rocks,
    to watch the ferry, in the sun;
And you cross the ferry with the naked people, go up the tropical lane
Through the palm-trees and past hollow paddy-fields where naked men
    are threshing rice
And the monolithic water-buffaloes, like old, muddy stones with hair on
    them, are being idle;
And through the shadow of bread-fruit trees, with their dark green,
    glossy, fanged leaves
Very handsome, and some pure yellow fanged leaves;
Out into the open, where the path runs on the top of a dyke between
    paddy-fields:
And there, of course, you meet a huge and mud-grey elephant advancing
    his frontal bone, his trunk curled round a log of wood:
So you step down the bank, to make way.

Shuffle, shuffle, and his little wicked eye has seen you as he advances
    above you,
The slow beast curiously spreading his round feet for the dust.
And the slim naked man skips down, and the beast deposits the lump of
    wood, carefully.
The keeper hooks the vast knee, the creature salaams.

White man, you are saluted.
Pay a few cents.

But the best is the Pera-hera, at midnight, under the tropical stars,
With a pale little wisp of a Prince of Wales, diffident, up in a small pagoda
    on the temple side
And white people in evening dress buzzing and crowding the stand upon
    the grass below and opposite:
And at last the Pera-hera procession, flambeaux aloft in the tropical
    night, of blazing cocoa-nut,
Naked dark men beneath,

And the huge frontal of three great elephants stepping forth to the tom-
   tom's beat in the torch-light,
Slowly sailing in a gorgeous apparel through the flame-light, in the front
   of a towering, grimacing white image of wood.

The elephant bells striking slow, tong-tong, tong-tong,
To music and queer chanting:
Enormous shadow-processions filing on in the flare of fire
In the fume of cocoa-nut oil, in the sweating tropical night,
In the noise of the tom-toms and singers;

Elephants after elephants curl their trunks, vast shadows, and some cry out
As they approach and salaam, under the dripping fire of the torches
That pale fragment of prince up there, whose motto is *Ich dien.*

Pale, dispirited Prince, with his chin on his hands, his nerves tired out,
Watching and hardly seeing the trunk-curl approach and clumsy, knee-
   lifting salaam
Of the hugest, oldest of beasts, in the night and the fire-flare below.
He is royalty, pale and dejected fragment up aloft.
And down below huge homage of shadowy beasts, bare-foot and trunk-
   lipped in the night.

Chieftains, three of them abreast, on foot
Strut like peg-tops, wound around with hundreds of yards of fine linen.
They glimmer with tissue of gold, and golden threads on a jacket of
   velvet,
And their faces are dark, and fat, and important.
They are royalty, dark-faced royalty, showing the conscious whites of
   their eyes
And stepping in homage, stubborn, to that nervous pale lad up there.

More elephants, tong, tong-tong, loom up,
Huge, more tassels swinging, more dripping fire of new cocoa-nut cressets
High, high flambeaux, smoking of the east;
And scarlet hot embers of torches knocked out of the sockets among bare
   feet of elephants and men on the path in the dark.

And devil dancers, luminous with sweat, dancing on to the shudder of
     drums,
Tom-toms, weird music of the devil, voices of men from the jungle singing;
Endless, under the Prince.

Towards the tail of the everlasting procession
In the long hot night, more dancers from insignificant villages,
And smaller, more frightened elephants.

Men-peasants from jungle villages dancing and running with sweat and
     laughing,
Naked dark men with ornaments on, on their naked arms and their
     naked breasts, the grooved loins
Gleaming like metal with running sweat as they suddenly turn, feet apart,
And dance and dance, forever dance, with breath half sobbing in dark,
     sweat-shining breasts,
And lustrous great tropical eyes enveiled now, gleaming a kind of laugh,
A naked, gleaming dark laugh, like a secret out in the dark,
And flare of a tropical energy, tireless, afire in the dark, slim limbs and
     breasts;
Perpetual, fire-laughing motion, among the slow shuffle
Of elephants,
The hot dark blood of itself a-laughing, wet, half-devilish, men all
     motion
Approaching under that small pavilion, and tropical eyes dilated look up
Inevitably look up
To the Prince,
To that tired remnant of royalty up there
Whose motto is *Ich dien*.

As if the homage of the kindled blood of the east
Went up in wavelets to him, from the breasts and eyes of jungle
     torch-men.
And he couldn't take it.

What would they do, those jungle men running with sweat, with the
     strange dark laugh in their eyes, glancing up,

And the sparse-haired elephants slowly following,
If they knew that his motto was *Ich dien*?
And that he meant it.

They begin to understand,
The rickshaw boys begin to understand;
And then the devil comes into their faces,
But a different sort, a cold, rebellious, jeering devil.

In elephants and the east are two devils, in all men maybe.
The mystery of the dark mountain of blood, reeking in homage, in lust,
    in rage,
And passive with everlasting patience,
Then the little, cunning pig-devil of the elephant's lurking eyes, the
    unbeliever.

We dodged, when the Pera-hera was finished, under the hanging, hairy
    pigs' tails
And the flat, flaccid mountains of the elephants' standing haunches,
Vast-blooded beasts,
Myself so little dodging rather scared against the eternal wrinkled pillars
    of their legs, as they were being dismantled;
Then I knew they were dejected, having come to hear the repeated
Royal summons: *Dient Ihr!*
Serve!
Serve, vast mountainous blood, in submission and splendour, serve royalty.
Instead of which, the silent, fatal emission from that pale shattered boy
    up there:
Ich dien.

That's why the night fell in frustration.
That's why, as the elephants ponderously, with unseeming swiftness
galloped uphill in the night, going back to the jungle villages,
As the elephant bells sounded tong-tong-tong, bell of the temple of blood,
    in the night, swift-striking,
And the crowd like a field of rice in the dark gave way like liquid to the dark
Looming gallop of the beasts,

It was as if the great bare bulks of elephants in the obscure light went
 over the hill-brow swiftly, with their tails between their legs, in
 haste to get away,
Their bells sounding frustrate and sinister.

And all the dark-faced, cotton-wrapped people, more numerous and
 whispering than grains of rice in a rice-field at night,
All the dark-faced, cotton-wrapped people, a countless host on the shores
 of the lake, like thick wild rice by the water's edge,
Waiting for the fireworks of the after-show,
As the rockets went up, and the glare passed over countless faces, dark
 as black rice growing,
Showing a glint of teeth, and glancing tropical eyes aroused in the night,
There was the faintest twist of mockery in every face, across the hiss of
 wonders as the rocket burst
High, high up, in flakes, shimmering flakes of blue fire, above the palm
 trees of the islet in the lake.
O faces upturned to the glare, O tropical wonder, wonder, a miracle in
 heaven!
And the shadow of a jeer, of underneath disappointment, as the rocket-
 coruscation died, and shadow was the same as before.

They were foiled, the myriad whispering dark-faced cotton-wrapped
 people.
They had come to see royalty,
To bow before royalty, in the land of elephants, bow deep, bow deep.
Bow deep, for it's good as a draught of cool water to bow very, very low
 to the royal.

And all there was to bow to, a weary, diffident boy whose motto is
 Ich dien.
I serve! I serve! In all the weary irony of his mien—*'Tis I who serve!*
Drudge to the public.

I wish they had given the three feathers to me;
That I had been he in the pavilion, as in a pepper-box aloft and alone
To stand and hold feathers, three feathers above the world,

And say to them: *Dient Ihr! Dient!*
Omnes, vos omnes, servite.
Serve me, I am meet to be served.
Bring royal of the gods.

And to the elephants:
First great beasts of the earth
A prince has come back to you,
Blood-mountains.
Crook the knee and be glad.

Commentary • *Elephant*

P. "Elephant" is literally a long description of the reception for the Prince of Wales who'd come to Sri Lanka, presumably in the 1920s because he's described as a boy. It's a description of the elephants and a description of the Prince (which is not very flattering). There is a play upon his motto *"Ich dien,"* ("I serve"), and in the end Lawrence says it would have been better if *he* had received the three feathers: "that I had been he in the pavilion." This is surely the culmination of Lawrence; in other words "Serve me! . . . I need to be served, Being royal of the gods." Lawrence. What do you make of that one?

B. Quite a statement. Lawrence is worthy of being served but this . . . He claims a royal knowledge that this dispirited, tired-out white man of the West doesn't possess.

P. I would guess this to be about 1926 or 1927. Lawrence was with a friend of his at the time, and he was about to be very, very ill. But I find "A prince has come back to you, / Blood-mountains. / Crook the knee and be glad" difficult to take.

B. Lawrence as Prince. Yes, I fear that that is so. He feels that they should be bowing and scraping to him rather than to the Prince of Wales.

P. He had a pretty good opinion of himself.

B. I'll say . . . this certainly is stretching it a bit. It's an extraordinary ending. Hyperbolic as hell. Even the elephants should bend, should acknowledge.

P. Well, the elephants are bending their knees to the Prince, of course, but he's sick of all this stuff.

B. The Prince is "burnt-out" as it were but as you've just pointed out, Lawrence was too. He probably had less than three years to live. This is an astonishing personal vision, an inflation of personality. Remarkably self-serving.

P. Quite so.

B. What do you make of it?

P. I'm a little stumped by it. But the description of the elephants and of the whole scene is magnificent.

B. What is the "Pera-hera"?

P. A special ceremony put on, of course, for the benefit of the Prince.

B. There Lawrence describes the relationship between the natives and the elephants; they may both be on bended knee but, secretly, they both have a deeper sense of life than the dispirited Prince?

P. Undoubtedly; it is a scene of tremendous vitality . . .

B. They have a patient waiting quality about them, both native and elephant, presumably waiting for the white man, for white society, to collapse. Like North American aboriginals.

P. Where do you get that? Look, the poem is not at all consistent. Here he is at first a scared little man and in the end he's saying "Bow down to me." This inconsistency rather spoils the poem for me.

B. Yes, it seems to me to be flawed because of that inconsistency of character of the speaker of the poem. Lawrence feels he should get the feathers because he should be served by both man and beast.

P. He would appear to . . .

B. There's no irony here . . .

P. There doesn't appear to be. And elephants were not the first great beasts of the earth. Even before the dinosaurs, there were great beasts . . .

B. The poem offers a tremendous description of the midnight ceremony however. It has great value for that alone. But Lawrence's vision of himself intrudes on this. I admire him for having the guts to write it and risk ridicule, but it is an amazing performance. Yet, it's an image that fuels the fire of his critics. It plays right into their hands, it serves their purpose gloriously. A god-like Lawrencean image—Lawrence as Buddha—terribly inflated, egotistical.

P. It certainly gives his critics plenty of ammunition. In some sense Lawrence was a monster of egotism. In another sense he was a very human small man all his life. There are theories about illness that say that the ill person compensates for his or her illness, sometimes by creation, sometimes in other ways. This may have been what Lawrence was doing here.

B. Unconsciously.

P. This may have been just a lapse. In *The Psychic Mariner*, Tom Marshall's excellent book on Lawrence's poems, he says that Lawrence "is not really interested in political institutions and methods; nor more impressed by Mussolini's attempts to restore grandeur to Italy than he was by the Prince of Wales. He certainly would have been appalled by Hitler. What he wanted was not a political revolution but a revolution for life, a re-instatement of pride, a change of heart." It seems to me that he mistook the very accoutrements of royalty as if they were part of his desire for "change of heart." But it isn't, obviously.

B. Tom Marshall talks about those two upsetting final stanzas as Lawrence making a better show of monarchy, as being about the establishment of a new order, a hierarchical order, a revolution of life, and all of that is good and true except that Marshall is ignoring the line "I wish they had given the three feathers to me," and he is further ignoring the first person singular, which occurs three times in one stanza. Marshall has paid no attention to the fact that Lawrence has replaced the Prince of Wales.

P. Marshall sees Lawrence in this ideal state as an artist's dream kingdom like Yeats's "... Byzantium." But to bow the knee to Lawrence here is nothing like these references.

B. No, it isn't. Surely here we have the problem with Lawrence's conception of Rananim, Lawrence's ideal community or paradise. The problem was it had to have Lawrence at the head of it. Nobody else. Probably no other members. "Elephant" is about the reason why Rananim never came into being. Because others who would have come to this community of artists somewhere in the world—Taos perhaps—would indeed have to serve the Lawrence of this poem.

P. Lawrence was a flawed genius in many ways; a magnificent poet, a magnificent prose writer, but, nevertheless, he wasn't a saviour of the world—as he would have liked to have thought himself.

B. Maybe the nature of genius is that it is always flawed.

P. Lawrence had some reason for ego, of course.

B. Oh, my, yes.

P. Not in this respect, however. I don't necessarily think that writers make very good leaders of men. But the sheer ego repels me in this poem. This is ego exemplified. Yet the first part of the poem describing the ceremony is magnificent.

B. Which is why we've included it here. But the poem could have ended without these last two stanzas. It could have ended with "Drudge to the public." But the last two stanzas are typical of the recklessness of genius. The adventurer that Lawrence was takes the poem beyond the edge of the world and off the deep end.

P. It's typical of the genius, it's also typical of his own ego that having been an inconsequential boy and young man he develops quite an ego. I'm not suggesting he didn't have some justification in possessing an ego but to take it quite this far is a little silly.

Whales Weep Not!

They say the sea is cold, but the sea contains
the hottest blood of all, and the wildest, the most urgent.

All the whales in the wider deeps, hot are they, as they urge
on and on, and dive beneath the icebergs.
The right whales, the sperm-whales, the hammer-heads, the killers
there they blow, there they blow, hot wild white breath out of the sea!

And they rock, and they rock, through the sensual ageless ages
on the depths of the seven seas,
and through the salt they reel with drunk delight
and in the tropics tremble they with love
and roll with massive, strong desire, like gods.
Then the great bull lies up against his bride
in the blue deep bed of the sea,
as mountain pressing on mountain, in the zest of life:
and out of the inward roaring of the inner red ocean of whale-blood
the long tip reaches strong, intense, like the maelstrom-tip, and comes
        to rest
in the clasp and the soft, wild clutch of a she-whale's fathomless body.

And over the bridge of the whale's strong phallus, linking the wonder of
        whales
the burning archangels under the sea keep passing, back and forth,
keep passing, archangels of bliss
from him to her, from her to him, great Cherubim
that wait on whales in mid-ocean, suspended in the waves of the sea
great heaven of whales in the waters, old hierarchies.

And enormous mother whales lie dreaming suckling their whale-tender
        young
and dreaming with strange whale eyes wide open in the waters of the
        beginning and the end.

And bull-whales gather their women and whale-calves in a ring
when danger threatens, on the surface of the ceaseless flood
and range themselves like great fierce Seraphim facing the threat
encircling their huddled monsters of love.
And all this happens in the sea, in the salt
where God is also love, but without words:
and Aphrodite is the wife of whales
most happy, happy she!

and Venus among the fishes skips and is a she-dolphin
she is the gay, delighted porpoise sporting with love and the sea
she is the female tunny-fish, round and happy among the males
and dense with happy blood, dark rainbow bliss in the sea.

Commentary • *Whales Weep Not!*

P. It's occurred to me that what we're doing to Lawrence is what Lawrence is doing to whales here: he's appreciating them. This poem also connects with the earlier poems in its open ending. They're all so open; he's leaving so much to the reader, it seems to me.

B. The poems are wide-open; it's one of Lawrence's great qualities in these poems and elsewhere. His best poems have a sweep and a depth that few other poets achieve. Not only the endings are open; sometimes it appears that every line the man wrote was open. Every line seems to open to a world that is larger than the world being talked about. In this poem he begins by talking about the sea, then moves quickly into the whales, then to the "sensual ageless ages" through the "depths of the seven seas ... " This is an extraordinary probing beneath the surface of things, a cosmic exploration or journey. Whether he sets out from "the molten centre of the earth" or from "the depths of the seven seas" this is extraordinary imaginative leaping for a Nottingham miner's son, as you earlier called him. It's interesting that having shunned his father's life, and despised the life around him when he was a child, this man—in his own unique poetic way—has also gone into the centre of the earth, following in the footsteps of his father, in a way that his father and his father's fellow miners could never imagine.

P. I'd like to say a word about his father. I think that in the early part of his life Lawrence was on his mother's side. But in later life when he realized he condemned his father—probably unjustly—he changed his view. His father was an interesting man and I don't think Lawrence despised his father in his later life at all.

B. Virtually every line in this poem opens to a resonance that speaks of a larger life. Few poets, if any, match him in this.

P. By the way, among the whales Lawrence mentions are hammerheads, which are actually sharks. Do you notice also, when he's talking about the sexual intercourse (shall we say) of whales, he's making it religious. He's referring to archangels and other levels of angels. What is passing between the whales is somehow holy.

B. For Lawrence the sexual act was holy. Lawrence's whole philosophy, his approach to life, was based on that. So when the whales link up here . . .

P. He carries it through to human beings too.

B. All living things.

P. All living things. The sexual act is allied to the creative act for Lawrence. They both partake of each other.

B. This is the "fathomless body" he speaks of, and it was something he worshipped. It was the pulse of his creativity. Perhaps—because of his illness—a transference had occurred for him from his life to his art. Is this what gives such depth, such insight, to the later poems? I'm so taken by his amazing ability to link things. As in "the beginning and the end" of the fifth stanza, of earth, of time, life itself.

P. Do you notice how he brings in Greek mythology?

B. And a Roman reference. And the order of angels, you mentioned? And it's all brought in, apparently effortlessly—you don't feel any intellectual straining here as you often do when other poets and writers do this. It's unconscious perhaps?

P. This is the man that the critics claim lacks form, has no background in writing or literature. It seems to me they're a little nuts to think that. How could you read his work and make those statements?

B. I have a question, Al. Since Lawrence works so well for you, why doesn't Whitman?

P. One thing antagonizes me about Whitman. His idea of camaraderie, of walking down the road, slapping everybody on the back, hailing everybody, that sort of thing. I like whomever I like. I don't want to like everybody. Besides, I don't have the time anyway. It strikes me as silly. Remember the line that Auden cut out of his poem: "We must love one another or die." And it's what Whitman is saying. Something very similar. And I don't like it. Whitman wanders around intermittently in his poems. Now Lawrence, to some degree, got that habit from Whitman. Some of Lawrence's poems are very long and we've said so, but in many of those long poems there are some unforgettable lines and phrases. Taken out of context they can occasionally sound commonplace but a line like "I didn't know his god," referring to the fish, sets up a strange reverberation in my mind.

B. I agree. I think Lawrence accused Whitman of a "false exuberance" and of being "too superhuman," though he admired him for his energy, his vitality. Very American; very un-Canadian. Is Lawrence's long line the same as Whitman's? Lawrence wrote how it all depends on the pause, the natural lingering of the voice according to the feeling ... that hidden emotional pattern that makes poetry, and not the obvious form.

P. I don't think Lawrence's lines are nearly as long, though I haven't looked at Whitman lately.

B. I haven't either.

P. I don't like him.

B. You think that Lawrence's line is doing a different thing?

P. It is. He learned from the sort of freedom that Whitman has. I'm not dismissing Whitman or anything like that, I'm just saying there are some things about him I don't like. I've been accused of being like Whitman and that antagonizes me. For the most part Whitman is a poet of praise. But Lawrence is a far more perceptive and intelligent poet; he sees farther and deeper into almost anything you can name. Whitman let his mind run free in the way that Jack Kerouac writes books.

B. It was Truman Capote who said once that Kerouac's work was not writing but typing. But didn't Lawrence have Whitman's male sense of camaraderie?

P. Yes, he did. I don't have it. Not the same way.

B. With Lawrence it doesn't get into the poems to nearly the same extent as with Whitman.

P. It gets into the novels, of course.

B. But it's not often in the poems, and not at all in the poems we've chosen here. In the poems he's totally one with the subject, he becomes what he's writing about.

P. Homosexuality is in *Women in Love* ...

B. Yes. And ties in with Whitman there.

P. A lot of people accused Lawrence of being homosexual. An incipient homosexual, I guess.

B. In life, when things really got close, Lawrence turned away from the very male camaraderie that he espoused.

P. Middleton Murry, for instance. Lawrence had a very religious attitude toward Murry, he felt Murry would betray him. It's odd, that's a pretty grandiose concept.

B. It is. But he had a grandiose concept of everything. He wanted to live in a community of fellow beings who would live in a way that made them fully sexual, fully aware, like these poems. And yet, when that seemed like a possibility, Lawrence was the last guy in. Lawrence couldn't live with anybody, nobody could live with Lawrence. How could you?

P. Do you recall Charles Bukowski's poem about the last generation, which included Lawrence? He said Lawrence was bad-tempered and so on, words to that effect.

B. Apparently he was. And couldn't live with anyone, whereas Whitman had companions, good friends. Lawrence couldn't stand people when they got too close to him; the very thing he was asking for.

P. That's right, it's a strange business. But the poems are written quite differently than the novels. The camaraderie of male to male is not in the poems.

B. No, here the camaraderie is between the male of our species and the natural world. That's a camaraderie that Lawrence can tolerate.

P. When he went to the Etruscan tombs he gave credit to the Etruscans for being a much more natural people than the Romans.

B. The natural world, these whales, this is Lawrence's community, this is his true communion.

P. And it is also, as we mentioned earlier, a religious poem. The business of the phallus passing into the female and what passes back and forth in that phallus is something religious that has to do with the Cherubim and the Seraphim and so on.

B. That's the religious, holy communion of community that Lawrence really wanted, and the irony is it's not possible with humans, only with animals. But there is something else I want to talk about regarding this poem, and that is Lawrence's attitude toward the feminine, which, in this poem, seems to be that the female should be most happy when she's procreating, serving the purpose of life and evolution, and that that is her sole responsibility, her purpose. It's not a stance that has endeared him to feminists.

P. He doesn't bar males from their role in procreation though.

B. No, but Lawrence feels fundamentally that the male leads and the woman follows and that this is her role. *And* that she is most happy when she does this.

P. Regarding human relations between male and female, I don't think that question is ever going to be settled. There's always going to be an argument.

B. Of course, the conflict is eternal. But given contemporary gender politics, the last stanza of "Whales Weep Not!" is amazing. The female is in a subservient role, extremely limited, and not merely in that role but loving it "round and happy among the males."

P. A lot of women won't read Lawrence because of this attitude.

B. Young women begin with Lawrence and are often swept away by what appears at first to be his liberating sexuality and unfettered freedom. It's only later they find his views on the feminine terribly constricting.

P. It's in the novels, of course.

B. And in this poem.

P. I have to admit that I think his attitude toward women leaves something to be desired.

B. I'll say . . .

P. The male-female war will always go on. And I'm not sure it's a bad thing either. As long as it's not carried into violence, of course.

B. It's a natural conflict that is part of life itself.

P. I don't think that Lawrence's attitude is either right or correct. Let's just leave it at that.

B. One other thing. I don't usually experience any difficulty with

Lawrence's language but the inversion in the second stanza "and in the tropics tremble they with love" is awkward and unlike Lawrence. It's archaic.

P. Oh, yeah, I agree.

B. It's one of a few lines where this happens ...

P. Well, he may do it again but if he does, the phrase is so striking that you don't even notice it.

B. Everywhere else in the poem the man sings.

P. If he makes a mistake like that you can think of it as being similar to when you read Yeats: you're not bothered by it at all, though the line you've pointed out is indeed pretty awkward. But in the largeness of our hearts we forgave Yeats for his rhyming metric "Mad as the Mist and Snow."

B. Absolutely. And we forgive Lawrence in the same manner.

P. Yes.

B. I'm completely taken by the openness, the sweep of the poem. The recent death of Allan Ginsberg has brought much renewed praise for his "Howl" and some other poems of his but, migod, Lawrence had such a magnificent sweeping line of such grandeur half a century ago!

P. Oh, lord, Lawrence had a much larger sweep than Ginsberg ever thought of having.

B. And Ginsberg took from Lawrence—and of course from Whitman—that incantatory buildup of line upon line. Here, Lawrence achieves that same effect—the poem grows larger and larger and comes at the reader like some tidal wave. It's a great notion, it's a natural motion for Lawrence; he's riding the crest of it in this poem. And he takes the reader along too.

Fish

Fish, oh Fish,
So little matters!

Whether the waters rise and cover the earth
Or whether the waters wilt in the hollow places,
All one to you.

Aqueous, subaqueous,
Submerged
And wave-thrilled.

As the waters roll
Roll you.
The waters wash,
You wash in oneness
And never emerge.

Never know,
Never grasp.

Your life a sluice of sensation along your sides,
A flush at the flails of your fins, down the whorl of your tail,
And water wetly on fire in the grates of your gills;
Fixed water-eyes.

Even snakes lie together.

But oh, fish, that rock in water,
You lie only with the waters;
One touch.
No fingers, no hands and feet, no lips;
No tender muzzles,
No wistful bellies,
No loins of desire,
None.

You and the naked element,
Sway-wave.
Curvetting bits of tin in the evening light.

Who is it ejects his sperm to the naked flood?
In the wave-mother?
Who swims enwombed?
Who lies with the waters of his silent passion, womb-element?
— Fish in the waters under the earth.

What price *his* bread upon the waters?

Himself all silvery himself
In the element
No more.

Nothing more.

Himself,
And the element.
Food of course!
Water-eager eyes,
Mouth-gate open
And strong spine urging, driving;
And desirous belly gulping.

Fear also!
He knows fear!
Water-eyes craning,
A rush that almost screams,
Almost fish-voice
As the pike comes . . .
Then gay fear, that turns the tail sprightly, from a shadow.

Food, and fear, and joie de vivre,
Without love.

The other way about:
Joie de vivre, and fear, and food,
All without love.

Quelle joie de vivre
Dans l'eau!
Slowly to gape through the waters,
Alone with the element;
To sink, and rise, and go to sleep with the waters;
To speak endless inaudible wavelets into the wave;
To breathe from the flood at the gills,
Fish-blood slowly running next to the flood, extracting fish-fire;
To have the element under one, like a lover;
And to spring away with a curvetting click in the air,
Provocative.
Dropping back with a slap on the face of the flood.
And merging oneself!

To be a fish!

So utterly without misgiving
To be a fish
In the waters.

Loveless, and so lively!
Born before God was love,
Or life knew loving.
Beautifully beforehand with it all.

Admitted, they swarm in companies,
Fishes.
They drive in shoals.
But soundless, and out of contact.
They exchange no word, no spasm, not even anger.
Not one touch.
Many suspended together, forever apart,
Each one alone with the waters, upon one wave with the rest.

A magnetism in the water between them only.

I saw a water-serpent swim across the Anapo,
And I said to my heart, *look, look at him!*
With his head up, steering like a bird!
He's a rare one, but he belongs ...

But sitting in a boat on the Zeller lake
And watching the fishes in the breathing waters
Lift and swim and go their way—

I said to my heart, *who are these?*
And my heart couldn't own them ...
A slim young pike, with smart fins
And grey-striped suit, a young cub of a pike
Slouching along away below, half out of sight,
Like a lout on an obscure pavement ...

Aha, there's somebody in the know!

But watching closer
That motionless deadly motion,
That unnatural barrel body, that long ghoul nose, ...
I left off hailing him.

I had made a mistake, I didn't know him,
This grey, monotonous soul in the water,
This intense individual in shadow,
Fish-alive.

I didn't know his God,
I didn't know his God.

Which is perhaps the last admission that life has to wring out of us.

I saw, dimly,
Once a big pike rush,
And small fish fly like splinters.
And I said to my heart, *there are limits*

To you, my heart;
And to the one God.
Fish are beyond me.

Other Gods
Beyond my range ... gods beyond my God ...

They are beyond me, are fishes.
I stand at the pale of my being
And look beyond, and see
Fish, in the outerwards,
As one stands on a bank and looks in.

I have waited with a long rod
And suddenly pulled a gold-and-greenish, lucent fish from below,
And had him fly like a halo round my head,
Lunging in the air on the line.

Unhooked his gorping, water-horny mouth,
And seen his horror-tilted eye,
His red-gold, water-precious, mirror-flat bright eye;
And felt him beat in my hand, with his mucous, leaping life-throb.
And my heart accused itself
Thinking: *I am not the measure of creation.*
This is beyond me, this fish.
His God stands outside my God.

And the gold-and-green pure lacquer-mucous comes off in my hand,
And the red-gold mirror-eye stares and dies,
And the water-suave contour dims.

But not before I have had to know
He was born in front of my sunrise,
Before my day.

He outstarts me.
And I, a many-fingered horror of daylight to him,
Have made him die.

Fishes
With their gold, red eyes, and green-pure gleam, and under-gold,
And their pre-world loneliness,
And more-than-lovelessness,
And white meat;
They move in other circles.

Outsiders.
Water-wayfarers.
Things of one element.
Aqueous,
Each by itself.

Cats, and the Neapolitans,
Sulphur sun-beasts,
Thirst for fish as for more-than-water;
Water-alive
To quench their over-sulphureous lusts.

But I, I only wonder
And don't know.
I don't know fishes.

In the beginning
Jesus was called The Fish . . .
And in the end.

Commentary • *Fish*

B. One thing that amuses me when I read "Fish" is how all these poems emanate from a single vision of Lawrence's, a vision of the diversity of life, of the divisions of life, between the primordial oneness of animals and things and the conscious life of man.

P. And the fact that they're individuals. I also feel that he's saying in the middle of this poem someplace that you are in a different element than air and that fish never really touch each other, physically or emotionally.

B. That's right, this is not like the tortoise poems, not like "Tortoise Shout" which we'll come to later; this is a different thing, in a different element.

P. The tortoise that Lawrence describes that we talk about is out of water, on the land.

B. But in the water there's a different nature at play. Notice also that, unlike "Snake," where he debates about whether or not he should kill the snake, and experiences that dichotomy between the two sides of himself, as in "Mosquito"; here he kills the fish.

P. Undoubtedly fishing for food, I would think. But what I'm interested in here is the repeated line "I didn't know his God." It seems to me a hinge line.

B. Yes, the pivot of the poem.

P. Also, I'm not sure what he means by: "Which is perhaps the last admission that life has to wring out of us."

B. I was going to ask you about that. Could it be, regarding Lawrence's vision, acknowledgement that there are other lives, other worlds, other gods, is the last and final thing we can say about life. It's a deep truth about life that Lawrence early on arrived at by experience, and having arrived at it, for him it was the last and greatest thing he could discover.

P. Well, he has talked about other gods before, of the Etruscans and the gods of other peoples. And he did that when he was in Mexico, reading of the Aztecs and the Mayans. So this isn't anything new, particularly, it's something that he's been going on and on about for a long time.

B. Exactly my point. Whether consciously or unconsciously—and I'd suspect the latter—Lawrence has an incredibly unified vision of human life and other lives and other worlds. It's extraordinary how often it recurs in his best poems.

P. He places himself ... there are certain kinds of animals that he feels a kinship with and describes them and feels them, and he may even get sentimental about them at times ...

B. Sometimes ...

P. But not about fish, particularly. He was fond of the tortoise of course, but fish, no.

B. When I first re-read "Which is perhaps the last admission that life has to wring out of us," it struck me that that would have been a more than suitable ending for the poem and that most poets would have been more than satisfied to end the poem there, if they'd got there at all. I don't think too many of us would have.

P. Do you know anything about the actual ending?

B. All I can think of is that, for Lawrence, in some sense, being a spiritual being, Jesus would have represented a pure immortal soul. And Jesus is like the fish in that he too was caught and died.

P. I can't think of Lawrence as being religious in any conventional sense. Would he have thought that there is a God, and a Jesus Christ, who was crucified on the cross? Did Lawrence believe all that?

B. He uses the images of the crucifixion and Christ in his poems. Is the Christ figure only an image for Lawrence?

P. I don't know. He leaves it pretty ambiguous.

B. Yes, but he does seem to hold to the Christian tenet. And his belief seems orthodox, simply because he mentions Christ and the crucifixion so often.

P. I still think he's using them simply as images.

B. I don't believe he'd use them so often if they were only images. He wouldn't use such images so often *unless* he believed in them. At the same time he goes way beyond gods for "others." In the deep unconscious of its being, the fish has a creator. Jesus was often represented by the fish, as a giver of life, and there is the suggestion here that if we could return to the fish, return to our primordial state or at least recognize it, be aware of it, we would again "swim" in a larger life than the one that we now lead.

P. You think there's a suggestion of that? Where do you find it?

B. In the tenor and tone of the whole poem. There is worshipping here of the fish and its natural element. The fish is unconscious and—being unconscious—the fish is whole, is one. He says this in a line. And we, humankind, have gotten away from that in our lives. So Lawrence's worship of animals and of those that lead a more primordial life is a criticism of us. That we've gotten far away from our sources, from the essence of life itself.

P. I certainly agree with you that we have, but I don't think there's a worship of animals, I'd choose the word fellowship.

B. Perhaps. But I feel it's much more than that.

P. You're talking of Lawrence's "oneness" with all things, but he is not one with the "Fish," he is saying "I didn't know his God, / Which is perhaps the last admission that life has to wring out of us." I'm not sure what he means; you're saying you have an idea but, aaah, there are alien things, there are things one doesn't understand, there are all sorts of things one doesn't understand about life, and if you believe ... of course I don't believe that the fish had a god in any way the same way that humans believe they have a god ...

B. No, no, of course ... but something ...

P. But there are some principles, some spirit, something that Lawrence felt that fish had.

B. Well, yes, but something created this thing ...

P. Aaah, you're talking about it as if there is a Creator, a God? You're getting into something else here, I can see that. Because if you get into that, then you're asking who created our supposed God ...

B. Lawrence envies the "wholeness" of the fish, he envies its "oneness," he envies the "oneness" of the fish's life when he writes: "Dropping back with a slap on the face of the flood and merging oneself / to be a fish. . . . "

P. There is something about being in water, the water connects you with other fish, whereas air doesn't, in the same way. And, therefore, fish are in some way more closely related to each other than humans are, except he talks about the copulation of fish here, and that they never really touch, they just touch water.

B. So there's something elemental about water, it goes beyond the other elements, there's something even more primordial, more ancient, about living in water.

P. Primordial is first things, but why is water before everything else?

B. I don't know, but Lawrence seems to be suggesting that, no? That a different life emerges from, comes out of water.

P. "He outstarts me," meaning, I guess, that fish and the relatives of fish were here on earth before humans, before mammals, I presume he means. I feel we're falling short on this poem, somehow. Of course, humans, as amphibians, first come out of water.

B. I love the ...

P. I love the "slim, young pike, with smart fins / And grey-striped suit ... slouching along away below, half out of sight / Like a lout on an obscure pavement ... / Aha, there's somebody in the know!" He's making a joke of course. And it's funny.

B. Yes, yes and no. I mean here is somebody that has some knowledge that we don't have ...

P. But it's a joke. You don't think it's a joke?

B. Not the last line. The images are so exaggerated as to provoke laughter but I don't think "there's somebody in the know" is a joke.

P. You don't?

B. I think he's serious, despite the comic invention and exaggeration of his images.

P. I guess we disagree again.

B. Good.

P. Look at the next stanza right after the one we've been talking about: "I had made a mistake, I didn't know him." So he's saying that he made a mistake with that other stanza. That is a clever joke, I cannot possibly see it as anything else.

B. The images are comic, but the "somebody in the know!" has a double-edge to it, a double meaning, it's both comic *and* serious, he's saying, look, this fish has a sense of things . . .

P. A sense of what things?

B. A sense of things that Lawrence doesn't have, a sense of life.

P. Sure, he's said that all through the poem. There are many things we don't know about life, we don't know about fish in particular.

B. Because you felt we weren't "grabbing hold" of the poem, I wanted to mention Lawrence's brilliant imaginative detail here, as in "the gold-and-green pure lacquer-mucous comes off in my hand" line. It's exquisite. Maybe one way one grabs hold of the poem is to relish and read aloud such brilliant images. Lawrence always gives the reader the sense that the full experience has been felt, absorbed in his being. What a beautiful line.

P. The whole passage is beautiful.

B. The experience is made transparent, and handed directly to the reader in a way that few poets have ever been able to accomplish.

P. But first you have to see these things before they become "transparent." He conceives them.

B. Exactly. Lawrence had that vision. He had that genius, an imaginative genius.

P. It's genius that can place himself in the same position as a fish or kangaroo. There's a sympathy that allows him to temporarily be what he is talking about.

B. It begins as a sympathy and becomes an empathy.

P. Should we look up "Jesus was called the fish"? Do you know that passage at all?

B. No.

P. No, I don't either.

B. I wouldn't have thought it's a quotation, but simply a general reference, to the biblical image.

P. Well, it's in upper case letters ... Here, Lawrence causes the fish to die, and he's done the same thing before, in other poems. Though he didn't feel that about the mosquito.

B. No, but he considers the possibility in "Snake," doesn't he. And then rejects it.

Invocation to the Moon

You beauty, O you beauty
you glistening garmentless beauty!
great lady, great glorious lady
greatest of ladies
crownless and jewelless and garmentless
because naked you are more wonderful than anything we can stroke—

be good to me, lady, great lady of the nearest
heavenly mansion, and last!
Now I am at your gate, you beauty, you lady of all nakedness!
Now I must enter your mansion, and beg your gift
Moon, O Moon, great lady of the heavenly few.

Far and forgotten is the Villa of Venus the glowing
and behind me now in the gulfs of space lies the golden house of the sun,
and six have given me gifts, and kissed me god-speed
kisses of four great lords, beautiful, as they held me to their bosom in
     farewell
and kiss of the far-off lingering lady who looks over the distant fence of
     the twilight,
and one warm kind kiss of the lion with golden paws—

Now, lady of the Moon, now open the gate of your silvery house
and let me come past the silver bells of your flowers, and the cockle shells
into your house, garmentless lady of the last great gift:
who will give me back my lost limbs
and my lost white fearless breast
and set me again on moon-remembering feet
a healed, whole man, O Moon!

Lady, lady of the last house down the long, long street of the stars
be good to me now, as I beg you, as you've always been good to men
who begged of you and gave you homage
and watched for your glistening feet down the garden path!

Commentary • *Invocation to the Moon*

B. What do you make of Lawrence's invocation?

P. It is an appeal to the moon as if the moon were a woman, to help Lawrence in his extremity because this, I believe, was written at a time when he was feeling very ill, was very ill. He's giving the moon both feminine powers and metaphysical powers and saying how wonderful the moon is. And that she has the power to help him, isn't that how the poem strikes you?

B. Absolutely. And, further, that she is even more wonderful than any conceivable human connection between male and female.

P. Perhaps he's saying that, I dunno.

B. "Because naked you are more wonderful than anything we can stroke."

P. Okay, but it strikes me as a very odd line too, because it includes all creatures.

B. Odd-good or odd-not-so-good?

P. It's a little extreme, frankly.

B. Is the poem a premonition of death?

P. Oh, yes, meaning I think I'm about to die. It is possible also that he is appealing to all the gods, not just the moon. In "There Are No Gods" he states, from his point of view, there are gods and he echoes that here. And he's appealing directly to the gods but to the moon first and foremost.

B. She becomes the "garmentless lady of the last great gift." The gift of death? Is he so ill that he sees death as a gift? As I grow older I can understand that. This is what Lawrence liked about Whitman; that he went to the edge and had the courage to look over into the abyss. Irving Layton believed this made Frost a minor poet—that he got to the edge but didn't dare look over.

P. What is the gift?

B. Normally I'd say poetry but I believe it to be death. In the final stanza she's the "lady of the last house." This poem is a prayer . . .

P. I'd say it is . . .

B. A prayer to the moon for the passage into death. For that last journey. For safe passage.

P. As the Egyptians took their boat, their ship of death, to the underworld. Interesting Lawrence wrote a poem with that title.

B. So Lawrence invokes the moon to watch over his passage from life into death. It's a plea to her to "be good to me now."

P. He's going into the unknown and that being so . . .

B. As a result of what we've said about "Invocation . . . " does it stand up as one of the great Lawrence poems?

P. I think it's his twelfth best in the present company. You judge a poet by his best stuff and this is one of them.

B. He knows that he's near death. He appeals to the moon as a poet— not because he thinks it's going to do any good. What a plea: "set me again on moon-remembering feet / a healed, whole man."

P. This poem to me seems somewhat exaggerated and when I come to a line like "Because naked you are more wonderful . . . " it jars on me. I know that he was near death when he wrote the poem—or believed that he was—and I can sympathize with that, feel that, but here he piles exaggeration upon exaggeration. One of the good things about Lawrence and one of the bad things about Lawrence is that sometimes he gets carried away.

The Man of Tyre

The man of Tyre went down to the sea
pondering, for he was Greek, that God is one and all alone and ever more
      shall be so.

And a woman who had been washing clothes in the pool of rock
where a stream came down to the gravel of the sea and sank in,
who had spread white washing on the gravel banked above the bay,
who had lain her shift on the shore, on the shingle slope,
who had waded to the pale green sea of evening, out to a shoal,
pouring sea-water over herself
now turned, and came slowly back, with her back to the evening sky.

Oh lovely, lovely with the dark hair piled up, as she went deeper, deeper
      down the channel, then rose shallower, shallower,
with the full thighs slowly lifting of the water wading shorewards
and the shoulders pallid with light from the silent sky behind
both breasts dim and mysterious, with the glamourous kindness of
      twilight between them
and the dim blotch of black maidenhair like an indicator,
giving a message to the man—

So in the cane-brake he clasped his hands in delight
that could only be god-given, and murmured:
Lo! God is one god! But here in the twilight
godly and lovely comes Aphrodite out of the sea
towards me!

Commentary • *The Man of Tyre*

B. This seems paired with "Invocation to the Moon". They're both invocations to the feminine but here the invocation works brilliantly.

P. "Invocation" ... is a little verbose and, as I pointed out, exaggerated. "The Man of Tyre" seems right, the phraseology. That seems to be all that needs to be said.

B. This is a glorious celebration of womanhood.

P. And religion. Because it's a religious poem, it makes the feeling itself religious.

B. That's a beautiful way of putting it. The celebration of the woman becomes religious.

P. He brings in religion, femininity, beauty, and sex. The whole works.

B. It's all one for Lawrence. The language, oh, the language in the third stanza is magnificent; in her, in her elemental femininity, giving a message to the man. It's a glorious painting of Frieda, no?

P. I think "Giving a message to the man" is amusing.

B. Well, Al, Frieda was probably the only woman for Lawrence. The language in that third stanza is not so surprising but it all comes together brilliantly.

P. The words themselves, even in the thoughts, the phraseology is not so startling, as you say, but ...

B. Often, in Lawrence, it's the cumulative effect, the incantatory build-up of line upon line.

P. He does something similar in "Bells," which we talk about next.

B. You see this more and more in the longer poems. Ginsberg attempted this.

P. Yes, but he piled lines upon lines to such a degree that they toppled over.

B. The technique can easily break the poem apart. But the poems we've chosen don't topple over.

P. Maybe the Americans worship Whitman so much that when they saw that Ginsberg was influenced by Whitman they liked him for that. And of course it was also what Ginsberg said. Sometimes Americans like to hear bad things about themselves. They're most interested in other people's opinions about them, so long as they can forgive the bad opinions.

B. Lawrence could have gone on and on in the third stanza but he uncharacteristically contains himself in the formal shape of the poem. "The Man of Tyre" is held beautifully. It's held within the poem, in a way that is spoken about in the last stanza.

P. There is *some* exaggeration but it's exaggeration that you can live with. I almost recall the first time I read this poem years ago and thought "what a lovely poem," and you read it many more times and in a commonplace voice because somehow Lawrence makes it commonplace and wonderful at the same time.

B. Your reading in that commonplace voice is so good for the poem because that's what the language calls for, you get rid of that jarring and rhyme of the "sea . . . me" so close together at the end. Read your way one is not disturbed by the ending.

P. I didn't even notice it. Also it's a little story. It's a story . . .

B. Meaning . . .

P. Well, let's go through it. Incidentally, do all Greeks "ponder"? It makes you wonder. Anyway, it's giving him credit for being a philosopher.

B. In Greek mythology they do.

P. And philosophy too.

B. A minor cavil. I wish to hell we could get rid of Lawrence's extreme overuse of the exclamation point! But they don't bother you, eh?

P. I don't even think of them. Why do they bother you?

B. They suggest a weakness of expression, a weakness in the language which the punctuation is attempting to alleviate. If he had the language that he really wanted, the exclamation marks would be unnecessary. Maybe he doesn't have the language he wants, maybe it's not possible for words to convey what Lawrence often feels.

P. I read the poems for the sense of them, I pay no attention, unless it's a line break.

B. I guess I feel the language *is* good enough, and therefore it doesn't need them. He used them a lot and I don't think they're necessary.

P. No, I don't either. Sometimes Lawrence's whole language is exclamation.

B. Right. You don't need the marks. However, it's a minor cavil.

P. You like the word "cavil."

B. I seem to have just discovered it. It's just that these poems are so great, it's sometimes necessary to make some minor criticism, just to keep sane. And they could be better. But I don't mean to nitpick. "The Man of Tyre" is a great homage to the feminine.

P. Yes, though strongly religious because it makes female-male relations religious.

B. For Lawrence they were.

Bells

The Mohammedans say that the sound of bells
especially big ones, is obscene;

That hard clapper striking in a hard mouth
and resounding after with a long hiss of insistence
is obscene.

Yet bells call the Christians to God
especially clapper bells, hard tongues wagging in hard mouths,
metal hitting on metal, to enforce our attention . . .
and bring us to God.

The soft thudding of drums
of fingers or fists or soft-skinned sticks upon the stretched
        membrane of sound
sends summons in the old hollows of the sun.

And the accumulated splashing of a gong
where tissue plunges into bronze with wide wild circles of sound
and leaves off,
belongs to the bamboo thickets, and the drake in the air
        flying past.

And the sound of a blast through the sea-curved core of a shell
when a black priest blows on a conch,
and the dawn-cry from a minaret, God is Great,
and the calling of the old Red Indian high on the pueblo roof
whose voice flies on and on, calling like a swan
singing between the sun and the marsh,
on and on, like a dark-faced bird singing alone
singing to the men below, the fellow-tribesmen
who go by without pausing, soft-foot, without listening,
        yet who hear:
there are other ways of summons, crying: Listen! Listen!
        Come near!

Commentary • *Bells*

P. I'm completely bewildered by this poem. I find it very difficult to talk about because the poem says all the things that need to be said. You've got to almost be there to hear everything going on. How can you talk about this?

B. I'm not sure one should. I remember when we first looked at this poem together, you said that even to suggest talking about "Bells" seems to take away something from the poem. But I do have some questions. Why is the sound of the bells "obscene"?

P. I don't know. I think when I read "that hard clapper striking in a hard mouth / and resounding" it seemed sexual.

B. It's an obvious sexual image but why isn't it simply sexual, why is it obscene? I think Lawrence was always repressed, despite his ongoing attempts to throw off his English background and upbringing. You can never entirely rid yourself of that kind of thing and he never did. Couple that with his terribly debilitating illness and you get a man looking at sexuality from the outside—at least after the first few years with Frieda. The sexuality he wanted but could no longer have becomes obscene. The early Lawrence would have celebrated this sound.

P. Yeah, he would have. It's as if he's going back on what we think he is. The poem then becomes archaeological, as if he's going back into time itself.

B. The poem moves from pure sound through religion, the archeological, the primitive, wildlife . . .

P. He's making a Grand Tour.

B. And condensing so much. In a single stanza he moves effortlessly from North Africa to New Mexico in one line!

P. You mean his mind should be tired out instead of his feet.

B. He might be tiring out the reader . . .

P. He doesn't me.

B. No, he doesn't, but that's what's so remarkable, that's what's so "unspeakable" about the poem. He covers such vast time and territory.

P. It's a fascinating poem and I don't exactly know why.

B. We don't have to know why. There is a more natural bell in nature, and Lawrence's movement is fascinating; the way he moves from the religious human experience into nature—which for Lawrence was more natural. Did the external rhyme of the last two lines affect you?

P. I didn't even notice it.

B. He places the last phrase as far away from the "hear" as possible.

P. I think that's probably the reason. The rhymes are quite a ways away in sound, if not in actual lines.

B. Yes, it's far enough away in sound, you're right.

P. What's he getting at with "there are other ways of summons"?

B. It's amazingly mysterious. I don't know. The feeling he establishes in the poem becomes a resonance, a ringing in the mind, a numinous sounding.

P. Is he saying this at the end? Is Lawrence himself speaking here?

B. I took it to be Lawrence.

P. That last line seems to come from a long way off in time.

B. He wants to set up with the reader a resonating sound that resounds back centuries. And into the future. All over the world. Ways of people being summoned.

P. I'm dissatisfied with myself. The poem makes one feel the bells themselves, the ringing sound.

B. Perhaps this is what Auden meant by "transparency." That Lawrence achieves a clarity here that's so clear that you can't say anything about it, in a critical sense. One can only—and should only—experience the poem. The poem just is.

P. Maybe. I think Auden meant the meaning of the poem. What he was talking about. The thing itself. "Kangaroo" for instance. He saw the kangaroo—that's the transparency. But here the meaning is not so transparent. We don't know what he's talking about, we don't know what he's getting at at the end. What is he doing talking about all the ways bells are used by different people? That's not so transparent. It's hypnotic, that's what it is.

B. There's a mystery here we're not getting and I'm not sure we're intended to "get it."

P. It's as if Lawrence's own feelings were reflecting the sound itself.

Tortoise Shout

I thought he was dumb,
I said he was dumb,
Yet I've heard him cry.

First faint scream,
Out of life's unfathomable dawn,
Far off, so far, like a madness, under the horizon's dawning rim,
Far, far off, far scream.

Tortoise *in extremis*.

Why were we crucified into sex?
Why were we not left rounded off, and finished in ourselves,
As we began,
As he certainly began, so perfectly alone?

As far, was-it-audible scream,
Or did it sound on the plasm direct?

Worse than the cry of the new-born,
A scream,
A yell,
A shout,
A pæan,
A death-agony,
A birth-cry
A submission,
All tiny, tiny, far away, reptile under the first dawn.

War-cry, triumph, acute-delight death-scream reptilian,
Why was the veil torn?
The silken shriek of the soul's torn membrane?
The male soul's membrane
Torn with a shriek half music, half horror.

Crucifixion.
Male tortoise, cleaving behind the hovel-wall of that dense female,
Mounted and tense, spread-eagle, out-reaching out of the shell
In tortoise-nakedness,
Long neck, and long vulnerable limbs extruded, spread-eagle over her
    house-roof,
And the deep, secret, all-penetrating tail curved beneath her walls,
Reaching and gripping tense, more reaching anguish in uttermost
    tension
Till suddenly, in the spasm of coition, tupping like a jerking leap, and oh!
Opening its clenched face from his outstretched neck
And giving that fragile yell, that scream,
Super-audible,
From his pink, cleft, old-man's mouth,
Giving up the ghost,
Or screaming in Pentecost, receiving the ghost.

His scream, and his moment's subsidence,
The moment of eternal silence,
Yet unreleased, and after the moment, the sudden, startling jerk of
    coition, and at once
The inexpressible faint yell—
And so on, till the last plasm of my body was melted back
To the primeval rudiments of life, and the secret.

So he tups, and screams
Time after time that frail, torn scream
After each jerk, the longish interval,
The tortoise eternity,
Agelong, reptilian persistence,
Heart-throb, slow heart-throb, persistent for the next spasm.

I remember, when I was a boy,
I heard the scream of a frog, which was caught with his foot in the mouth
    of an up-starting snake;
I remember when I first heard bull-frogs break into sound in the spring;
I remember hearing a wild goose out of the throat of night

Cry loudly, beyond the lake of waters;
I remember the first time, out of a bush in the darkness, a nightingale's
piercing cries and gurgles startled the depths of my soul;
I remember the scream of a rabbit as I went through a wood at midnight;
I remember the heifer in her heat, blorting and blorting through the
      hours, persistent and irrepressible;
I remember my first terror hearing the howl of weird, amorous cats;
I remember the scream of a terrified, injured horse, the sheet-lightning,
And running away from the sound of a woman in labour, something like
      an owl whooing,
And listening inwardly to the first bleat of a lamb,
The first wail of an infant,
And my mother singing to herself,
And the first tenor singing of the passionate throat of a young collier,
      who has long since drunk himself to death,
The first elements of foreign speech
On wild dark lips.

And more than all these,
And less than all these,
This last,
Strange, faint coition yell
Of the male tortoise at extremity,
Tiny from under the very edge of the farthest far-off horizon of life.

The cross,
The wheel on which our silence first is broken,
Sex, which beaks up our integrity, our single inviolability,
      our deep silence,
Tearing a cry from us.

Sex, which breaks us into voice, sets us calling across the deeps, calling,
      calling for the complement,
Singing, and calling, and singing again, being answered, having found.

Torn, to become whole again, after long seeking for what is lost,
The same cry from the tortoise as from Christ, the Osiris-cry of
      abandonment,

That which is whole, torn asunder,
That which is in part, finding its whole again throughout the universe.

Commentary • *Tortoise Shout*

P. This is quite a long poem but it doesn't topple over. It gets stronger as it goes on because it's talking about the strangeness of the tortoise shout in the midst of copulation and Lawrence is likening it to an awful lot of other things—all the things he's heard: sounds of things, people, animals, in extremity. The poem moves from strength to strength.

B. You've touched on one of the reasons why we've chosen this select group of poems and not others. Because in some of the other longer poems we've left out, they topple over, as you said, from exaggeration, from extension of the line and the language.

P. That's his method that he got from Whitman, though Whitman goes on in the extreme, extreme, extreme, hyphenated extreme. But Lawrence doesn't go on to quite that extent. It should be remembered that "Tortoise Shout" is the last of a series of tortoise poems that say many things about the tortoise and humanity. It's essentially about screwing, fucking in other words. It seems to me that the words act out the sexual act. And it's also a commentary on the act of copulation. And, of course, tortoises—along with a lot of other animals—are also our ancestors. When you think that the evolution of human beings goes on in the human womb—all the way from the beginning, from the one-celled egg right on up to us. The opening stanza here re-enacts the beginnings of the human race, as in the second stanza. It's a re-enactment. Then he talks about "tortoise *in extremis*." The third stanza's impossible because, obviously, there has to be some method of procreation but, nevertheless, it is saying that the sexual act is also a form of torture. I *think* it says that.

B. This is the cry of sexuality and its necessity. It can be a burden, especially for the males. But it's a great poem for several reasons: the openness of the form, the variation of short and long line (migod, he's *so* free with that—how I envy him), lines that run off the page followed by two-word lines, the whole rhythmic shape of the poem.

P. You're finding it new even though you read it before?

B. Yes. And that's a further quality of Lawrence's poetry. I often find

Lawrence new. He offers a new experience each time you come to the poem—just like sex. But there's something else going on, Al. He speaks of the experience but then further extends the poem by going back into his own memory in the second part and recalls all the other cries he's heard . . .

P. . . . *in extremis.*

B. Yes; cries of nature.

P. It's as if he's going back to the beginning of human life.

B. First his life and then life itself. But the end of the poem is quite different. What he's asking for here is not simply a view of the sexual act as procreation but if we are to become whole human beings we can only become whole by "doing it" with someone else.

P. Obviously copulation depends on someone else.

B. That's obvious on the most literal level. But what Lawrence is calling for here is a wholeness of soul, a coming together of two souls as one. And what he's saying is very politically incorrect for our times—he's saying one cannot be whole in one's life *unless* one is with another. I believe that to be true.

P. This reminds one, in a way, of Phyllis Webb's "Breaking." Except that I suspect like hell that she meant copulation, along with something even more important.

B. But here Lawrence affirms the necessity of copulation and procreation not as ends in themselves—as necessary as that may be—but because only with someone else can one become whole.

P. It goes beyond that even. He's saying that terror, fear, the pain of copulation is like giving up the human, like giving up one's personality by entering into another person.

B. Yes, literally and figuratively.

P. The scream of a frog is simple fear. And the process of copulation contains all other things he refers to here. Do the wild goose, nightingale, rabbit, heifer, cat, horse, lamb just sound like that or are they more deeply connected in some other way?

B. In order to become whole you have to be broken apart, as Webb put it.

P. But her breaking doesn't apply only to sexuality; I think she's aiming at much more than that and so is Lawrence.

B. We have to be humiliated and defeated before we learn ... She's aiming at the same essential fact as Lawrence. And it's one we don't like to acknowledge. The same paradox. The whole idea of Christ being broken in order for us to become whole. You have to lose yourself in nature, in the natural act.

P. Is Christ not the only one of the gods who dies and comes back to life? I don't know. One of the elements of a very well-known philosopher (I've forgotten his name) was the repetition of the death of all things and the rebirth in spring. There was a ritual death of a girl or a boy ...

B. Or the king himself had to die.

P. Or the king had to die. Aah, do you see all that as allied to this?

B. Yes.

P. Though I'm not sure Christ is the only god who is resurrected. We'd have to know our theology a little bit better. But this amounts to a resurrection.

B. In sexuality one loses oneself and one *has* to lose oneself—to become broken—in order to find a larger self beyond oneself. Do you know that recent song by Leonard Cohen where he sings of the bell having a crack in it and the defect in the bell is how the light gets in? That's the same thing.

P. There is a sense where, in copulation, it doesn't always result in resurrection: the queen bee ...

B. ... and the praying mantis who literally devours her partner.

P. There is a sense that in copulation—

B. One is dying.

P. One is dying. Yes.

B. The French phrase for it, *le petit mort*. That in the epiphany of ecstasy one experiences a little death.

P. All of the tortoise poems lead up to "Tortoise Shout."

B. Yes, the great paradox. In order to become whole you have to become the parts of yourself. And give up yourself.

P. What lovely lines.

B. And that this process continues even after death. That we continue to find our "whole again throughout the universe." What a magnificent affirmation of life. And the way he's able to hold such diverse images—such parts—together in a simple poem is magnificent.

P. And when he writes of "our silence first is broken" he means the same as our inviolability, our person, our selves, our soul, whoever we are.

B. Do these animals he writes about instinctively, intuitively know these things that we have to discover?

P. I don't think they *know* these things at all.

B. They simply live them?

P. They live them; for them it's instinct, it's feeling.

B. Surely that's what Lawrence is calling for from us.

P. I don't think the ordinary person ever thinks these things that we're talking about now. Undoubtedly people with some education have thought like this. But ordinarily one doesn't.

B. But Lawrence did. Always. He *felt* like this. That one should live this way. This is the kind of revolution he wanted. A revolution, an evolution of life that would change the way we live—

P. ... in which two whole persons, completely individual from each other would melt together and have congress with each other and become one—however briefly.

B. But in that brief moment, by becoming one, become whole in a way he or she or it could never be alone.

Lawrence's Shrine, Taos

Pines, snowpeaks, cedars, greasewood, the occasional cow.
It's German up here, all Baden-Baden
black forest & this absurd shrine
Brett & Angelo designed.

Lawrence, you'd hate it now. Young frauleins
with bulging thighs like twin burros
march up the mountain with one thing in mind
they come
up the switchback path
like avenging angels that can't
quit. They pause
only to taste the clear air at each hairpin twitch.
Even the ones that hate you love you Lawrence.
It's simply themselves they can't stand.

A southwester wells up
& shakes the scrawny pines into applause.
What Jim Beam I've saved flows
from the phoenix to your chiselled name. Christ
this is communion Lawrence, what
you believed you wanted,
Rananim in Taos, you & Frieda
alone on a mountainside.

Everywhere I speak to you the wind rises.
When I squeeze into your chair I feel
your gnarled fingers gripping the wood.
A coyote, caged on the hillside,
stalks forever back & forth
on his track a few inches from the fence.
The caretaker tells me nothing
ever happens here.

Further up the mountainside
your ghost whispers through the trees
urging me on. I walk behind the shrine
tracking the bittersweet smell of sulphurous spring.
I take hold of a bough.
It breaks. I'm pitched
among the pines at the foothills
of the Rockies, tableland
of Taos a desert plateau 9000 feet below. Like you,
I want to make the whole journey
down.

    —D.B.

In Etruscan Tombs

At Cerveteri the mossy stones
scare hell outa my unbroken legs
teetering along narrow masonry
or scrambling down dark tunnels
then back into sunlight
to escape the long sleep of the dead

(—and at this point
I cuss out D.H. Lawrence some more
the guy who got me into all this
on accounta my DHL obsession
and I'll send him a hospital bill
from the Etruscan Underworld
if I can just get his home address)

—and wondering if the Etruscans
were really the gentle souls
Lawrence fancied they were
while the ominous tombs surround us
buried bones and ornaments and stuff
still undiscovered by tomb robbers
or vanished into museums waiting
for us in Tarquinia and Volterra
room after room and sarcophagus
after sarcophagus each with stone
sculptures of their one-time
occupants leaning negligently
and invariably on their left elbows
in the customary eating position
when the stone was alive
all of them focusing blank eyes
in unison at gaping tourists
as if they cast uncanny spells
and forced visitors to join them
prisoners in glass cases

—but the tombs the dark tombs
tumbled heaps of earth and stone
and my fixation with Lawrence
propelling me onward
—thinking of the small dark men
who fought the Romans and lost
they left so little of themselves behind
except their blood in Tuscany
a great tide of blood
from a vanished race
flowing now in living veins
making everyone here slightly different
giving them a yearning feeling
in their hearts for what they can't remember
—and to understand that much
about them is very close
to having a million people
in my arms and hugging them

—clambering over the mossy stones
from sunlight into darkness
my own imagination so vivid
I half expect to encounter a little man
with red hair and bright blue eyes
wearing a slightly snappish expression
when I inquire about his latest book
he is continually re-writing
and together
we scramble out of the tombs
to follow the well-marked trail
leading back the way we came from
the way we came from

    —A.P.